MY HOLLYWOOD STORIES

ALSO BY ERIC MORRIS

No Acting Please (with Joan Hotchkis)
Being & Doing
Irreverent Acting
Acting from the Ultimate Consciousness
Acting, Imaging, and the Unconscious
The Diary of a Professional Experiencer
Freeing the Actor

AUDIO TAPES

The Craft of Acting
The MegApproaches
Imaging for Acting

THE ERIC MORRIS ACTORS WORKSHOP IS LOCATED AT:
5657 Wilshire Blvd. Los Angeles, CA 90036 (323)466-9250

Internet Web site
www.ericmorris.com

MY HOLLYWOOD STORIES

ERIC MORRIS

With Contributions from Others

ERMOR ENTERPRISES

Edited by Carin Galsett

Published by
Ermor Enterprises
8004 Fareholm Drive
Los Angeles, CA 90046

TABLE OF CONTENTS

INTRODUCTION

This book is a compilation of short stories and anecdotes from the world of show business, the film industry and television. A number of them come from my own experiences, things that happened to me; others were told to me by an actor, a director, or a producer friend of mine. Some are humorous, while others are spicy, sexy, interesting, or obnoxious. I truly believe that most of them are real. Every tale I write about that reflects a personal experience is totally true and honest. I have not changed or exaggerated any details of my own stories. The stories that were told to me by other people, however, may have been embellished somewhat. They are only as honest and truthful as the people who related them, so it is up to the reader to determine their veracity. I am sure that the hearsay stories might have undergone additions or deletions, but I have not printed anything that was not received from a reliable source. By way of a disclaimer, I have to say that some of the things I relate have been Hollywood folklore for many years and have been told and retold many times by many people, so please understand that if you have any doubts about the truth of a story, you can sprinkle it with a grain of salt.

You have all seen television shows and movies about the crazy and underhanded things that go on in politics. Well, Hollywood is very much like Washington, D.C., in that respect. During the period that followed World War II there was a blanket over Hollywood: It was the time of the Red Scare. People were searching for Communists everywhere, and the industry was a target of many of the right-wingers. The House Un-American Activities Committee, created to ferret out all of the so-called Reds and headed by Senator McCarthy, was responsible for ruining the lives of hundreds of actors, directors, and writers. The notorious "Hollywood Ten" were writers who were blacklisted and couldn't work in the film industry. Several of them wrote under assumed names.

Sex is a commodity in Hollywood, and many careers have been made by women lying on their back in service to fat, repulsive producers, who can only get laid because of their power to supply opportunities to desperate and hungry people. Those occurrences and hundreds more take place every day in Hollywood. For the most part they never break the surface, and they go unnoticed by the world.

So, you see, all of what will be related in this book is not funny. I share a little of what I know, not because I am angry or bitter; quite the contrary, I feel quite successful and accomplished in my profession and am not dependent on the insecure sycophants who are in a position to hurt people. The book is meant, not to be a Hollywood exposé, but essentially to enlighten and entertain. I have been an actor in Hollywood for sixty years and have been teaching acting for fifty-two of those years, so I have accumulated quite a few experiences in that time. Many of the stories and events related here will humanize iconic figures who until now have existed only on the screen, and quite a few are about older actors whom the younger readers of this book may be unfamiliar with. It is, however, important that Hollywood history should be known by actors and others who are interested in the evolution of the motion-picture industry. Those stories reflect a period in Hollywood which was the end of the studio system, a time when each of the major studios had a stable of famous actors under contract, whom they would at times loan out to other studios for a film. I am hoping that those tales will entice younger readers to explore the past and learn that the future is totally dependent on what came before. The past is prologue.

There was a TV show that aired sometime in the eighties or nineties called "The Naked City." The prologue I believe—a voice over—said, "There are eight million stories in the city. This is one of them." There are probably many more than eight million Hollywood stories. Here are some of them.

HI, DIDDLE DEE DEE, AN ACTOR'S LIFE FOR ME. IT'S A WONDERFUL LIFE?

TAKE FROM OUT THE POCKET THE GUN!

One of my very early acting jobs was a small part on a television show called "The Court of Last Resort," which focused on investigating prisoners who either had been unjustly convicted or had served a large amount of time and been rehabilitated. After the ordeal, or when it was obvious that they had paid their debt to society, they were freed.

My part was only in the teaser of the show. I was the young perpetrator of a crime that would send me to prison for many years. I was to enter a small grocery store with the intent of robbing it with a gun. I was supposed to come into the store—a set on a soundstage—look around, see the owner behind the counter, pull out a pistol and tell the owner to put up his hands. He was to reach for something under the counter, and I had to shoot him and run out of the store. The next scene is where I am being led to a prison cell. The guard locks the cell door; I turn around, and with a look of evil hatred, spit at him. The camera moves to my face, which morphs into the face of Vaughn Taylor, the actor playing the older me, the leading role. That is my entire part as written, and it only takes place in the few moments of the teaser of the show. Sounds like a simple obligation to address, right? Well, it may sound funny now, but at the time it was a fucking nightmare that haunted my acting career for years after.

The director, a man named Reginald Le Borg, was from Hungary or somewhere in middle Europe. His English vocabulary was extremely limited, and he should have been directing foot traffic in the outer reaches of Mongolia! He had the sensitivity of a dead pig and even less concern for the sensitivity of the actor.

I showed up on the set quite early that day, reported to the makeup person and was costumed in an outfit indigenous to the period: pants, a shirt, a necktie, a sports jacket, and a hat. When the time came to shoot the scene, I stood outside the door to the grocery store, waiting excitedly to hear "Action!" Everything was in place and everyone was quiet. A few minutes passed, and finally I heard a voice on the other side of the door shout, "Come, come." What was that? I wondered. A new way to call for action? So I entered, looked around, and immediately heard, "No, look to de right to dat pole over der, and den look to heem at de conter."

Take two: I made my entrance again and that time turned my head somewhat mechanically to look at the pole, thinking all the while that it was unnatural for a robber to look so far away from the proprietor. Again I heard a shout: "Cut! No, no, make it easy!" What the fuck did that mean? More natural?

Take three: Now rattled and uptight about every movement I was about to make, I entered the store again, turned my head to the right, saw the pole, looked at the proprietor, and reached into my pocket for a gun that was the size of a small cannon. Lo and behold, the hammer caught in the opening of the pocket and would not come out. Pulling on the jacket, I ended up lifting it up to the middle of my chest. "Cut!" came booming out from the other side of the set. Le Borg waddled over to me. "Vat's wrong?" he asked. "Can't you pull the gun out? Didn't you practice before showing up to the set, or are you really ignorant about guns?" I explained that the opening of the pocket was too narrow for me to get the gun out. He screamed for the costumer to come and fix it, while mumbling something in a foreign language under his breath. Ripping out the entire inside pocket of the jacket, the costume person did not in any way address the narrow opening, but I was too scared to say anything at that point, so we continued the scene from where I had to pull the gun out of my pocket.

Take four. That time the director said "Action." I reached into the pocket, but…surprise, surprise, the gun wasn't there. With no pocket left to hold it, it had moved into the lining of the jacket, all the way into the back. I reached into the lining and bent over, fishing for the pistol and looking like a contortionist. "Cut, cut, cut!" again came bellowing out. Le Borg walked over to me, slowly acknowledging to the entire crew what he had to put up with, and it was the best acting on the set that day! At that point I was so stoned with tension that everything and everyone seemed to exist on the other side of a long tunnel. When Le Borg reached me, I tried to explain, but my explanation fell on deaf ears. Looking into my eyes with such disgust it almost hit me in the face like a fist, he slowly said, "Take the gun from out de pocket and put into de belt!" So I put the gun in my waistband; but because the trousers were so loose, I had to thrust my stomach forward to hold the gun in place. I look nine months pregnant, I thought.

We did it again. By then I had lost count of how many takes this was, but I reached for the handle of the gun, pulled it up from my waist, and at the same time grabbed the bottom of my necktie. It went flying up, hitting me in the face. "Cut!" That time Le Borg really took the opportunity to play victim to the crew. Making eye contact with everyone, he dropped his shoulders, shrugging at the same time. Motionless and frozen, I just stood there. Again we started from where I was to take out the gun, but I forgot to push my stomach forward, so when I went to pull the weapon out, it slid down my leg on the inside of my trousers. I felt it hit my instep and watched it slither across the floor about five feet in front of me. Dead silence greeted me on the set, and for a moment I lost track of where I was—only for a fleeting moment, probably as a result of being in shock. That time the director moved more quickly towards me, and I could actually smell his anger as he lifted the gun and jammed it into my open hand.

We did the scene again for the umpteenth time. To my great relief I succeeded in getting the gun out and pointing it at the proprietor. Without any written lines, I was about to say, "Put your hands up," or "This is a stickup," or "Give me all your money," but instead I heard, "Say, 'Up, up'" so I reluctantly said, "Up, up," at which point the man behind the counter reached for something. "No, no," I heard. I stopped and looked in the direction of Le Borg, who screamed that that was the cue to shoot. As frightened as I was, I was at the end of the road with that guy, and I screamed back, "No, no? That's a cue to shoot? It sounded like a cue to stop what I was doing."

The second scene, where I was being led to my cell, fortunately went off without a hitch. The whole thing had been an indelible ordeal, which later affected a large part of my early career as an actor in Hollywood. Lynn Stalmaster, the casting director, received a negative report about me and of course didn't investigate any further, so he never called me again. Le Borg is probably dead by now, and even the Devil refuses to let him direct in Hell!

THAT'S NEXT WEEK'S SHOW

Victor Jory

Fortunately I also had successes in those early acting days. I was once hired to play a gas-station attendant on the series "Manhunt," starring Victor Jory. It was one of those police-detective shows. Victor Jory was a seasoned character actor, who had played a multitude of roles dating back to the forties, including Injun Joe in *The Adventures of Tom Sawyer.*

My character was being questioned about a car that had pulled into the station I was working at. Jory wanted me to describe the car and its driver. I had around ten lines about a big Chrysler Imperial that I was very impressed with. Jory asked me the first question, but it was not the question I had in my copy of the script. I looked at him without answering, so he repeated the question. "I'm sorry, Mr. Jory," I said, "but that is not my cue." He asked the second question, and again I could not respond, because again it was not my cue. Fred Jackman, the director, hurried over to see what the problem was, and lo and behold, after looking the script over, he discovered the mistake: they had sent me the following week's script, which also had a gas-station attendant in it!

In those days they would film a half-hour show in three days. We were there to shoot the scene and were therefore under the gun, so to speak. They brought the right script over, handed it to me and asked me how long it would take me to get the lines down; should they take a lunch break? I told them that I needed about fifteen minutes and I would have the lines. They were not convinced but said OK. I put the script on the hood of the car in the scene and memorized it in less than fifteen minutes. We shot the whole scene in one take, which thrilled everyone. Jory came over to me, shook my hand and told me that I was a real trooper.

WHICH HORSE WERE YOU SITTING ON?

Warren Oates

Warren Oates, a friend of mine, was a very interesting actor, who had quite a good career. He was in *Bring Me the Head of Alfredo Garcia, Ride the High Country, Two-Lane Blacktop, The Wild Bunch,* and a host of other films.

One evening, we were sitting in the Rain Check, an actors' bar and hangout on Santa Monica Boulevard. Warren was on his fourth or fifth beer and I was drinking a Coke. We were talking about the business, and I was telling him about my career and how hard it was to get work. I wasn't complaining, since I was fortunate enough in those early years to be able to book a part at least once a month and quite often twice. Of course, it was usually just for a day or two, although sometimes I would get a role that lasted for a whole week. Warren, on the other hand, was having a pretty successful career at the time, and he began to laugh, saying that he gauged his career on which horse he was sitting on. I didn't get it, so he explained: When he had started out, doing mostly westerns, he would ride into town with four other cowboy actors. He would be on the fifth horse from the camera. As time went on, he moved to the fourth horse, then to the third, and so on until he was on the first horse and had all the lines. "That's when I knew I had made it in Hollywood!" he concluded.

SO I'M NOT STRONG ENOUGH?

Linda Cristal

A number of years ago I was living in the Valley, in a place called Shadow Hills. It was very rural, and the streets right below us allowed the residents to keep horses—not on our block though; and since I didn't want to shovel horse-shit, that was fine with me. We had a three-bedroom house with a very large yard and a pool. At the time I had been teaching for just five or six years.

One Sunday I received a call from Linda Cristal, an actress in my class who had been starring in big Hollywood films and had also done some television. She was a very beautiful woman, with talent to match, and she had done some very impressive work in my class. She sounded a little frantic on the phone, and she asked me if she could come out to my house; it was really important! I told her that it was Sunday and that I was with my family, but she was relentless in her pleading, so I finally said yes. She arrived, parked her Jaguar in my driveway and rang the bell. When I opened the door, I was shocked at how disheveled she looked. It was as if she had just gotten out of bed, had jumped into her car and come over. My surprise at her appearance was due to the fact that she was always well put together, with not a hair out of place and wearing designer clothes and makeup that was artistically applied. I offered her some tea and we went out on the patio. She was frantic. I asked her what was going on, and she told me that she was up for the lead in a big television series that could run for years (for those people reading this who are not in the business, if a series runs for four or five years, just the residuals mean millions of dollars to the actors). She told me that she had been interviewed by the producer, who really liked her look and agreed that she was talented but felt that she might not be strong enough for the character, the wife of a rancher, a ballsy lady who ran things, cracked the whip and took no prisoners. She told me that she had a second interview the following day and that she didn't know how to convince the producer of her power. I thought for some minutes and then said, "Go in there tomorrow, clear his desk, turn over every chair in the office, wreck everything in sight, and then start yelling at him about what strength is. Overpower him!" She sat there looking at me incredulously and asked, "Can I really do that?" I told her that she had nothing to lose, since he had already just about made up his mind about her not being strong enough. The next afternoon she called me to tell me that she had indeed done everything I had suggested, and that when she was finished, she had stormed out of the office. On her way home she had been informed that she had gotten the part. The series, "The High Chaparral," ran from 1967 to 1971.

I DON'T THINK HE LIKES ME— IS IT METHOD OR MADNESS?

David Caruso

It was 1993, when the movie *Mad Dog and Glory* was being filmed. It had a celebrity cast: Robert De Niro, Uma Thurman, Bill Murray and David Caruso. At that time David Caruso was involved with a woman who was a good friend of my stepdaughter, Bridgett. Since he was having a problem with De Niro, as I was told, Bridgett, who had been exposed to me as a teacher for a number of years and knew how I worked, suggested that I might be able to help David, give him some advice about his difficulty. David called me and told me that he was having a tough time on the film. He looked up to De Niro and respected him but felt that De Niro really didn't like him. When they were not shooting a scene, Caruso would walk up to De Niro and try to start a conversation, but De Niro was having none of it and would simply walk away. David felt very hurt and rejected. I asked him to explain the plot and his character in relation to De Niro's and he told me: "Well, he is an older cop, and I am his younger partner, who admires and respects him and wants to be accepted in return. De Niro's character obviously does not care about or respect this wet-behind-the-ears rookie and avoids any deep involvement with him. My character nonetheless attempts to impress him and be liked by him. Throughout the entire film my character does everything he can to gain visibility and acceptance."

After listening to his description of their relationship, it was clear to me that De Niro was using his work to promote that relationship. Because I have a background in a similar acting approach, I suspected that De Niro was creating the reality of the relationship and continuing to promote those feelings throughout the filming in such a way that his reality would not be diluted by any fraternization off camera. Actually, when an actor is attempting to experience the reality of the character, he needs to support it organically while working with the material. After listening to David and knowing that he didn't understand what De Niro was doing, I gave him this advice: "OK, David, just keep trying to get him to like you. Be ingratiating, tell him a joke, be extra nice to him. Let him know how much you respect him, and follow him around, even when you are not shooting a scene. If you are hurt by his rejection, let it show a little subtly." He listened, thanked me and said he would try to do all of the things I had suggested.

About a month later David called me again. He was elated and told me that just after they had wrapped the last scene in the picture, De Niro had knocked on his dressing-room door, entered with two dozen roses and a magnum of champagne, hugged him and kissed him on the cheek. Then David asked me, "How did you know, Eric?" I told him that I understand and pretty much know how De Niro works. Had I made David aware of what De Niro was doing, it would have blown the whole thing for both of the characters. I believe that David is a serious and committed actor, and he has an impressive career. No way do I wish to diminish his talent, but his acting orientation was different, and he didn't understand the process De Niro was involved in.

It is not the first experience I have had with that phenomenon. I personally have used choices to encourage the reality to exist on and off camera and have a number of times been uncomfortable for the other actors I was working with. A number of years ago I had a role on the television series "Fame." I was playing a drama teacher who had come from another school to have his class participate in a performance competition. My scene was with the music teacher of the host school who had deliberately undermined my group and kept us from winning the competition. It was a deliberate and exceedingly unethical act. I had other scenes in the segment before my encounter with the music teacher. Knowing, however, how I was going to feel towards him, I started working for choices related to him right at the beginning of the segment. I steered clear of him and created my distaste and anger before doing the scene with him where I was angry and livid and emotionally attacked him aggressively. When we shot the scene, I opened up on him, which caused him to back away from me and ask me if I was angry with him. It stopped the scene, and I responded by saying, "Yes, I am angry at you and I am supposed to be." We tried it again, and it freaked him out. Again the director yelled, "Cut!" He then pulled me aside and told me that the actor playing the music teacher was actually a music teacher and not an actor, and he asked me if I could tone it down a little so he could do the scene. I did just that, but it wasn't nearly as good a scene as it could have been.

Another experience related to that phenomenon happened when I went to Hawaii to coach Tiana Silliphant, the wife of Stirling Silliphant, a very famous and successful writer who had written the miniseries called "Pearl" that was being filmed in Hawaii. I will talk more about that experience later in the book, but for now I will just mention that Tiana, who was in my class, got this very emotional part on the show. She wanted me to be there in Hawaii to coach her. While there observing the work, I noticed that Dennis Weaver, who was playing a chicken-shit colonel who seemed to hate everyone and was a cantankerous antisocial guy who refused to socialize with anyone, had actually created that behavior, much to the misunderstanding of many of the people involved in the film. He was doing what he felt he needed to do to promote the consistency of that reality. I knew it, and maybe some of the more experienced actors also did, but not everyone.

If an actor is committed to truth and wants to really create the experience, he or she must be courageous enough to run the risk of being misunderstood. Unfortunately, Method acting has many detractors and critics and has been controversial for decades because of ignorant practitioners who really do not understand the technique. Even great actors who do not understand the process have demeaned it.

BEING A BLACK ACTOR

I had just gotten out of the army and was chomping at the bit to reinvest in my acting career. My brother Phil, who was a producer and associate to Harry Belafonte, was in town. They were staying at the Ambassador Hotel, which hosted the famous Coconut Grove nightclub that every celebrity in Hollywood attended at one time or another. Phil invited me up to his suite to meet Harry, which I was excited about. When I entered the suite, Harry was on the phone. He was sprawled out on the couch in his underwear, feet up. He acknowledged me with a head nod, and I sat in a chair across from him. He was speaking to James Mason, with whom he had done a film. It seemed to be a really intimate conversation between two friends who obviously respected and cared for each other. When he said good-bye and put the phone down, he turned to Phil and with an understanding smile said, "You know what James said to me when I asked him what he was doing? He said, 'I'm walking around the house trying to convince myself that I am in great demand and that the phone is going to ring at any minute!'" They both laughed a very understanding laugh, one that I didn't comprehend at the time. It took me years to know what an actor experiences in the business, no matter how famous or successful he may be.

Harry and I chatted for a bit. He asked me about myself and what I was doing. I told him that I had just been discharged from the army, where I had had a great job being a disc jockey, and he asked, "Why didn't you stay in then?" I was hurt by the comment but realized that he didn't know that I was an actor and had by that time done about twenty-five Equity plays and a couple of movies.

Room service interrupted our conversation and delivered a breakfast fit for a king. Right behind the waiter, Sidney Poitier entered the room. Harry greeted him warmly and they sat on the couch talking. I was impressed, having seen Poitier in some films. I thought he was a very fine actor. During the conversation Poitier said that he got thirty thousand dollars a movie and that probably that was what he would have to settle for in his career. Thirty thousand dollars seemed an awful lot of money to me, when I would have been delighted with a steady one hundred dollars a week.

However, I did understand what Sidney was saying and how he felt about what was going on in Hollywood at the time. Not very many black actors were working in films in 1957, and there were few opportunities for them. James Edwards was the token black actor they used during the late forties and early fifties. Before him there had been Canada Lee, an incredible actor.

It was just before the civil-rights movement began to accelerate. Phil and Harry were very involved, and as a result I too became active in the movement. Looking back at the struggle I realize how far we have come since then, but maybe not far enough. Sidney Poitier went on to greater roles and certainly more money, as well as an Academy Award. Not only has his contribution as an actor brought respect for all actors, but he was also one of those black actors who paved the way for others like him.

JUST WHEN YOU BEGIN TO REALLY MAKE IT, YOU DIE

Hollywood is full of actors who spend their life chasing the brass ring, and then they die leaving their imprint on celluloid tucked away in some studio vault. As an actor pursuing a career, you die many times before the final curtain falls. There are so many tragic stories, far too many to record in one book, but I will attempt to mention a few.

I was living in Chicago, going to school, while my brothers were still living at home. Both of them were much older than I. Morrie was almost twenty years older, and Phil was fifteen years ahead of me. They were both in the theater. Morrie was an actor, while Phil was into the technical aspects of theatrical production. At various times one or the other would visit New York or Hollywood on an exploration trip, testing the waters so to speak. On those various sojourns they met other actors on both coasts and created a bond of friendship with them.

Morrie, who took the name Edmund Morris, befriended an actor, Philip Van Zandt. Their friendship lasted many years. Philip was a Hollywood actor, a day player who sometimes had a decent small part in a film. He amassed a résumé of seven hundred films but barely made a living in Hollywood. There were good times and bad times, a "feast and famine" career, as it is referred to. Philip would send Morrie thirty-five-millimeter clips of the movie scenes he appeared in. As a youngster, I was completely impressed by those clips: I had a brother who knew a movie actor, and I was holding a small piece of a real Hollywood film in my hand!

Flash forward: I was now in Hollywood to pursue an acting career and was encouraged to look up Phil Van Zandt. I was given his telephone number and street address and, after speaking with him on the phone, was invited to visit him. He lived in a small apartment very close to a freeway overpass. The place was dingy, dark, and littered with dirty clothes and empty whiskey bottles scattered all over the place. A woman was there, but I don't remember much about her, other than the fact that she was drunk and sprawled out on some pillows on the floor. Phil was lying on an old sofa that had seen better days and was wearing an undershirt that would have been better off in the washing machine. He was very nice. He greeted me as if he had known me for a long time, and he spoke very highly of my brother. I told him my story, and he listened with some interest but seemed very sad. In the next half hour he painted a dark picture of Hollywood. He told me that if there was anything else I could do other than pursue an acting career I should really consider it. I listened undaunted and knew in my heart of hearts that it would be different for me. Phil died shortly after my visit, broke and an alcoholic. He was found dead, probably on that sofa, with half a bottle of bourbon spilling what was left onto his chest.

So many tragic stories can be told by almost every actor who has ever been on this journey. I was in a taxi with Curt Conway and Dennis Patrick in New York. I was there to do a weekend workshop, but I don't remember where we were going. Somehow I had met Curt, and we were probably going to dinner. Dennis was a familiar face in the business. He had done films, television episodes and soap operas. At that moment he was bumping around in the back seat of that taxi, crying like a baby, in desperation about not having worked in some time. He told Curt that he had alimony payments, mortgage payments, and child-support payments and that he was stone broke! What was he going to do? My heart went out to him, but of course only a large part in a big movie would have solved his problems. Some years later Dennis died when his house was consumed by fire.

Sally Field

I was playing a small part in the film *Eye for an Eye.* I was a magazine journalist and had a scene with Sally Field and Beverly D'Angelo. We were waiting for the crew to set up the shot. Sally was knitting and behaving as if this was just another day for the movie star that she was. Beverly and I were talking, filling the time with stories about the neighborhood we lived in. Beverly lived across from me in the Hollywood hills. Sally asked me why I had come to California, and I said it was to pursue an acting career. She looked at me with an expression of great surprise, as if silently saying, You're kidding! I understood that response and was extremely hurt by it. To her I was just a day player, something like one cut above background atmosphere.

That experience was a karmic payback for me. Many years earlier I was playing Fred Barker in *Ma Barker's Killer Brood.* It was a leading role at an early time in my career. One of the other actors was talking to another guy and complaining about his acting career. I had seen him in small parts in western movies and would have never considered him as an actor. He didn't see my response, but it was exactly the same as Sally's reaction to me. I remembered that experience when Sally looked at me, and I felt hurt and ashamed at the same time. It was justifiable payback for being arrogant and an elitist, and I learned an important lesson that day.

Steve Inhat was an actor, one of those that people might recognize but not attach a name to and say, "Oh, there's that actor what's his name." I used to see him around town. We would pass each other in restaurants and make a hand gesture of recognition. We both frequented the Old World Restaurant on Sunset Boulevard, and occasionally I would take a moment and stop at his table, interrupting his reading of the trade papers. He was one of the lucky ones, or so it seemed. He worked in movies and television and saved all the money he could stash away from the parts he played. When he had amassed enough money, he started to make a film. He shot on weekends and whenever he could pay for the film stock. The film was called *Don't Throw Pillows into the Ring*, and when it was finished, Steve circulated it around town. A large producing organization saw it and gave him a three-picture deal to direct. I think he had already done one of those three films when he had a heart attack and died in a bathtub in Cannes. He was on his way to the big time and had just about reached middle age, and he was gone.

YOUR AGENT IS CALLING

Robert Christopher

We were sitting at a table drinking coffee at the French Market restaurant on Santa Monica Boulevard. Robert Christopher and I were talking about our exploits in show business. Robert, who just turned ninety and looks years younger, has acted in scores of films and was telling me about his role in *The Barefoot Contessa,* which he did many years ago. He also talked about Rome and acting in Europe, where he spent some time working in films. He always sits at the same table and is irritated if, when he arrives, other people are there. On Mondays the next larger table is occupied by what our group calls the "Mafia meeting." It consists of aging Italian actors who have worked in films over the years. Some of them owe their success to *The Godfather* saga. Like Schwab's Pharmacy in the old days, this restaurant is also an actors' meeting place, and quite often three or four other people join Robert, seeking a respite from loneliness. Not all of the people who populate that table are lonely, but being an actor is a lonely thing. Most of them are of the geriatric group, still hanging on to whatever work might come their way. Our conversations are about the business, or one of us might ask the others if they were aware a certain person had died and whether or not they knew him or her. Every once in a while a star's name comes up in the conversation, and there is always someone to comment on having worked in a film with him or her.

"I got a callback on the audition I went on last Tuesday," someone at the table said that day. "I really nailed it, but my agent said they went with someone younger!" Another person jumped into the conversation and told us that he had received a residual check for thirty-four cents. "You should frame it," I said. Robert laughed and told us that back in the days when he was still working as an actor he hadn't heard from his agent in months. He finally got a call from him saying that he was going out of business. That is not an uncommon thing. The agent I was once with had hired a new assistant, who, when I called to speak to my agent, didn't know who I was, which instilled great confidence in me!

People reading this book who are not actors might find it difficult to tune into an actor's consciousness. Acting is a profession unlike almost any other and it is therefore very difficult for "civilians" to understand us. Two actors who don't know each other can meet, look into each other's eyes, and without a single word uttered, get it!

MISADVENTURES IN A HOLLYWOOD APARTMENT BUILDING

The building was a rectangle in the center of Hollywood and probably held about eleven or twelve apartments, which surrounded a swimming pool that might have been thirty or thirty-five feet long. I lived in apartment 110, a one-bedroom on the ground floor very close to the pool. There was also a second floor with about six one- and two-bedroom apartments. I had recently been discharged from the army, was enjoying my newfound freedom, and had just purchased a brand-new 1957 red Corvette. I had saved up some money while in the army, and my wife had been working on the base I was stationed at, so between us we had enough for a good down payment on the car. I was ready to pursue my acting career. My wife got a nine-to-five job, and I applied for unemployment and hoped that my acting work would bring in a supplemental amount of money. At that time our rent was $110 a month. Remember, we are talking about 1958. My unemployment was $33 a week, and Jean, my wife, was earning $75 a week, so between us we could cover the rent, the car payment, food and other miscellaneous bills. Our income also afforded us the ability to go to dinner and a dollar movie once a week. I would get a day's work on a television series about once a month, which was a bonanza, the minimum daily rate for an actor being $90. If I was fortunate enough to get two days on a film, we were rich!

The building we lived in was occupied by a vast variety of characters. The apartment managers were an older couple named Drelich. She was a small, wizened woman, who scurried around picking up anything that was lying on the pavement and around the pool. Her husband, who was in his middle to late sixties, was very bald, with a narrow ring of gray hair just above his ears. He was slightly bent over and looked like some kind of bird searching for a worm to eat. His expression was always dire, and he often looked as if he had just pooped in his pants and was trying to escape the odor. The man was obsessed by his mortality and often talked about death.

On the second floor, in the apartment in the right corner, lived a very beautiful Hispanic high-class hooker. She always came down the stairs with a huge smile and dressed to the nines. I believe she applied full makeup and dressed as if she was going to a premiere even to go to the corner grocery. If I was at the pool, she made sure to look at me and give me a big smile. Even if I had wanted to, there was no way I could have afforded her services, but I was too proud to let her know that. Next to her, Lew, a middle-aged Jewish man, who was very affable, lived alone and would leave for work every morning with a sour look on his face, just as though he had swallowed a lemon. When he returned from work around six o'clock, he entered with a big smile. That, in a sense, told the whole story of his life.

On the other side of the pool lived a guy around twenty-eight or thirty years old, who was married to an attractive want-to-be model or actress. Every time she left the apartment to go somewhere, he would come out, look at her departing and check to see if there was anyone sitting around the pool who could witness his good fortune to be with such a beautiful woman.

Next to my apartment, in 112, was an older woman in her late fifties or early sixties, by the name of Hennie Mohr. She was the mother of a fairly well-known working actor, Gerald Mohr. He would visit her at least twice a week and sometimes even more often. Her life was totally dedicated to him. He was her reason for being alive and she doted on him, carrying food out to the pool and making sure that he was comfortable and that he had sunscreen on.

In the apartment directly above Hennie's, lived a couple of Holocaust survivors, a man and his wife who had met in a concentration camp and had later come together and married. In the apartment right next to them was another Holocaust survivor, a man in his middle fifties. Like all of the people in the camps during the war, he had numbers tattooed on his forearm. I remember seeing him poolside and noticing those tattooed numbers. A cold chill had run up my spine. It is one thing to have seen all those newsreels about the Holocaust and the emaciated prisoners behind the barbed wire, and another to actually sit next to one of them in the flesh.

My niece Bobby moved into the building with her husband, Lenny. She occupied the apartment directly above mine. Lenny, a short New Yorker about three inches shorter than Bobby, walked with an almost perfect posture and a little swagger. A meat cutter at a local market, he obviously thought he was a professional. He told me in a conversation that he was a "meat surgeon," at which point I asked to see his medical license—which went completely over his head!

Gerald Mohr

I don't know whether every apartment building in Hollywood had such a diverse clientele, but it was like living in a community. Gerald Mohr loved sitting poolside and "holding court." Since I was basically unemployed, I looked forward to sitting in the sun with him and talking about acting and the business. He loved the role of being the "movie star" impressing me, the young hopeful at the beginning of the journey. He spoke of the series he had done in Europe, "Foreign Intrigue," of how popular he was there, of the many films he had done in Hollywood and of how he was always approached for his autograph. He was full of interesting stories about his career and the actors he had worked with—which I found fascinating. He smoked very strong Egyptian cigarettes, strong enough to grow hair on your teeth, and in a single afternoon finished at least half a pack.

Barry Sullivan

One of the memorable and interesting stories he told me was about when he and Barry Sullivan were getting a blow job from two women who were under the table in the dining room of Sullivan's house. The two men were sitting there, talking about their last film experiences, while under the table two women of unknown origin were sucking their dicks. Gerald said that he and Sullivan went on with their conversation as if nothing was going on until, of course, the moment of "explosion," at which point the conversation was interrupted by the pure enjoyment of the experience. I naively asked if they had come at the same time, which made Gerald explode into laughter. He said he didn't remember, so I dropped the subject.

One afternoon we were at the pool reading the trade papers. No one else was there, except the man with the numbers tattooed on his arm. He was swimming awkwardly in the deep end of the pool, when he started to go under. He was splashing helplessly and was obviously in trouble. He went under and didn't come back up. I dove into the pool, came up under him, and was able to push him to the surface. He grabbed on to the coping and was able to crawl along it until he reached the ladder and got out of the pool. He was white as a sheet and stood there staring at me for a very long time. I think he was looking for a way to thank me but was unable to find any words. I smiled at him and climbed out of the pool. He walked up the stairs to his apartment. I thought what an irony it would have been if he had gone through the horrors of the Holocaust just to drown in a pool in Hollywood!

Living there was an endless adventure of one kind or another. My wife and I saved up enough money to purchase a twenty-eight-inch television set, a Magnavox, surrounded by ebony wood. It was very large, about five feet long and three feet deep. The screen was surrounded by a brushed gold border, and it was beautiful. We waited for over a month to get delivery, because Magnavox didn't make many sets in ebony, so it had to come from some place back East. The day finally arrived, and two delivery men brought the set into our living room and set it against the wall. I stood there admiring our purchase, anxious to see how clear the picture would be. One of the delivery men disappeared, while the other connected the cable and plugged it into the outlet. I turned it on, waited and…no picture! The screen was gray. We stood there waiting for a few minutes, when suddenly a small flame appeared behind the glass on the bottom of the screen. The flame grew in size until it was obvious that the fucking television set was on fire. The next few minutes were like what happens in a nightmare where you are being chased by a predator and you can only move in slow motion; your feet seem to be stuck in mud and you are paralyzed. Finally, we came to. We picked up the set, which seemed to weigh two tons, hurried towards the pool and threw it in. We stood there watching it bob up and down as it floated half submerged. A couple of the tenants came out and looked incredulously at the sight of the thing floating like a pool toy!

One evening as I was leaving the building, Anthony Quinn walked into the foyer. I recognized him immediately, and he saw that I did. His reaction was interesting, because he immediately responded by giving me his profile rather than his full face. If he could have morphed himself into another face, he would have. I wondered about his reaction, since he could have been visiting anyone in the building, but I instantly realized that he was there to see Gloria, the hooker on the second floor; and sure enough he headed right for that stairway. It was interesting seeing him, because just a couple of months earlier he had taken over Jeff Hayden's class, which I was attending at the time. Jeff was directing a TV show that day, so he had asked Quinn to teach the class. Steve Marlo was there to help Quinn, since he knew him and they had worked together before. I was sitting in the first row next to Steve, and Quinn was on his other side. Two actors were doing a scene on stage, when Quinn leaned over to Steve and made a very derogatory remark about the male actor. He said something about him, that he was "a lox" or something awful like that. I was within earshot, so I heard everything. I was shocked at his insensitivity. You would think that any actor in his position would be more sensitive and caring for another actor who is trying to grow and learn. I have always thought that Anthony Quinn was a very fine actor, but after that experience I thought that he was not a very good person.

WHAT'S IN A NAME?
AN ACTOR BY ANY OTHER WILL...

We have accepted that an actor's name is his name and that it may not even resemble the one he was given at birth. Actors' names have been changed for many reasons, and it would be interesting to find out what names they were really born with. When I started out to pursue my career in Hollywood, there was a very flamboyant agent named Henry Willson, who represented many of the actors who became stars. Almost every one of them had a name change, courtesy of Henry. I imagine that the chosen names were designed to create an image, possibly for the men a powerful masculine American image.

Here is a small list of actors whose names were changed:

John Wayne's name was originally Marion Robert Morrison.

William Holden's was William Franklin Beedle, Jr.

Jeffrey Hunter's was Henry Herman McKinnies, Jr.

Jeff Chandler was born Ira Grossel, and Mike Connors, Krekor Ohanian.

John Garfield's name was originally Jacob Julius Garfinkle; John Barrymore's was John Sidney Blythe, and Charles Bronson's, Charles Dennis Buchinsky.

Even I didn't escape the phenomenon. Born Fredric Stein in 1931 at the Mount Sinai Hospital in Chicago, I would have been happy using that name, but when I was just starting out my agent told me that it was "too ethnic," so my older brother, who had changed his name from Morris Stein to Edmund Morris, convinced me to take his last name, since he was going to introduce me to people in the industry who could help me get work. So I did. I kept half of my first name and changed the last to Morris, a name I have had for fifty-eight years.

ACTORS HELPING ACTORS
OR A FEW GOOD MEN...AND WOMEN

Hollywood has a reputation for being impersonal, with a short memory, little loyalty, and an emphasis on money. The operative questions are: Can money be made by courting an actor? What was the last thing that actor did, and was it successful? With incredible competition for booking roles, it is rare for actors to help other actors. The following stories are the exceptions.

FOR GOD'S SAKE, GET ME A PART IN *PORK CHOP HILL*

In 1959, two years after I got out of the army, I had an agent and was working as an actor about once or twice a month—a day here, two days there, and occasionally a whole week on a film. My agent, Betty Wookey, believed in me and would send me out on any audition I was physically right for. I had heard that they were casting for a film called *Pork Chop Hill,* and since I had been in the army and had already played at least half a dozen soldiers, sailors and marines, I thought, Great, I'm perfect for it! Almost everyone I knew was in the film, but Betty couldn't even get me an audition for it. I was really bummed. About a month after the film was finished, however, I got a call from her. She excitedly told me that they were adding additional scenes for the film and that she had gotten me two days in those scenes. I was elated! The part had no lines and could have been done by an extra, but for some reason they wanted two actors. It was shot on a soundstage at Samuel Goldwyn Studios. The set had a bunker, mountainlike terrain, and all the trappings of a hill in Korea. My costume included battle fatigues, a helmet, a rifle, and a backpack. I was totally familiar with the garb, since it was exactly what I had worn during basic training in the army. The director was Louis Milestone, an ancient man whose greatest claim to fame was that he had won an Academy Award for directing *All Quiet on the Western Front* in the early thirties. Gregory Peck was the star of the film, but it was also populated by many name actors: Woody Strode, Harry Guardino, Robert Blake, Rip Torn, and a host of others.

The first day on the set they had us jumping over trenches, running around the "mountain," taking cover behind structures, and so on. As I arrived on the lot on the second day, I was walking towards the dressing rooms, when I saw Gregory Peck walking towards me. "Good morning, Eric," he said. I was shocked that he not only knew my name but was very kind in greeting me. After all, I had only been on the film for one day, and I had a minuscule role! I responded by saying, "Good morning, Mr. Peck." He smiled and disappeared into his trailer. On that day of filming, most of the action took place in a bunker filled with soldiers. The enemy was using flamethrowers, and the flames were penetrating the bunker. At one point Gregory Peck put his arm around me, pulled me closer to him and said, "Eric, you are too close to the flames, and by being this close to me you will certainly be on camera." I was elated by his concern and kindness. As a side note, I have to say that Mr. Peck was a wonderful man, concerned about people and the world, a real humanitarian. Over the years I heard many people tell stories about his generosity and charity. The character he played in *To Kill a Mockingbird* was very much what he was as a man.

LET THE CAMERA SEE YOUR PRETTY FACE

In 1980 I was in a film produced by Roger Corman, *Battle beyond the Stars.* It was a futuristic science-fiction tale, based on *The Magnificent Seven,* about a benign planet, peace-loving by nature and without any weapons to defend itself against aggressors, and a larger warlike planet that desires to conquer and inhabit that smaller defenseless world. The aggressor was played by John Saxon as Sador. I played the role of Feh, a cowardly character who wants to surrender to the more powerful aggressor. The rest of the characters, led by Richard Thomas and Jeff Corey, want to resist being conquered. They send out pleas for help into the universe. A number of space junkies floating around in space vehicles, some of which have the weaponry to fight an aggressor, volunteer to help them, and the battle is on.

George Peppard

The volunteers included George Peppard, who was flying a ship that was supplying other planets with all kinds of necessary goods. His name was Cowboy. He was dressed as a cowboy and enjoyed listening to country music on his radio. Robert Vaughn played another volunteer who enlisted himself to help (incidentally Vaughn was also a character in *The Magnificent Seven*). A few others also took up the fight.

In one of the raging battles, Feh, my character, is shot in the back by one of Sador's ray guns and falls face down into the arms of Cowboy. George Peppard turned my body so that I would be facing the camera instead of having my back to it. I knew what he had done, and I thanked him after the scene was over. He winked and said, "We all have to look out for each other."

I LOVE LUCY—AND I REALLY DID!

In 1957 I spent ten weeks in Lucille Ball's workshop upstairs of the Coronet Theater. Without a doubt, those ten weeks constituted one of the greatest learning experiences of my life. We did scenes, which she watched and critiqued. She worshipped talent and was incredibly supportive of all the actors. My first experience seeing her standing in front of the group was awe inspiring. I was actually in the same room with Lucy! The lights shining down from the ceiling highlighted her red hair and created some kind of halo around her head. My heart was pounding so hard that I thought she might hear it; my palms were wet with anxiety and excitement. I was so nervous that I only heard every fourth word she said. It was our first session, and I wondered how I would ever be able to get up in front of her and act. In the second session I was somewhat calmer, but when she called my name, my heart jumped into my throat.

Lucille Ball

"Yes, Miss Ball, are you talking to me?" I responded.

She laughed and with a very kind smile said, "Yes, Eric, I was talking to you, and you can call me Lucy."

It was easier from that moment on. We connected, and she let me know that she was a real person, down-to-earth. There were about twenty people in the group. Besides doing scenes, they were very curious about Lucy and asked her a lot of questions, which she answered very openly and with disarming honesty. One of those people, an older woman—at least she was older to me, since I had just turned twenty-five—was June Levant, the wife of Oscar Levant. I realize that a lot of younger people will be reading this book and that most of them will not know who Oscar Levant was, so I'll digress for a moment and take this opportunity to educate them. Oscar Levant was a sardonic and very sarcastic humorist, who was sometimes caustic in his attempt to be funny. Also a concert pianist, he appeared in a number of films, including *An American in Paris* with Gene Kelly. June asked Lucy a number of questions, many of which we all wanted answers to; for example, "Lucy, didn't you ever go to a late-night party and then have to be on the set early the next day, possibly a little hungover? How are you then able to be Lucy?"

Lucy responded to the question as if she was happy it had been asked: "Well, I get into makeup and costume, and then I get with Vivian (Vivian Vance, her costar on the show), and we play, and very soon I get into the enchanted sense of play and can be Lucy."

Being an actor, I immediately understood what she meant. When I was doing summer stock, I would get to the theater early, turn on all the stage lights, stand in the blinding shower of light, look into the darkness where the audience would soon be, and fill myself with that sense of play, the joy of acting and feeling and the excitement that went along with it.

At that point in her life Lucy was at the top of her popularity. Her show was being aired all over the world and in many languages. She and Desi owned three movie studios, and several other television shows were produced by the Desilu organization. She told us a story that has stayed with me for fifty-five years and has kept me going as an actor during very rough times—you know, those times when you question what you have done with your life and ask yourself whether it was worth it. Lucy was a contract player at RKO in her younger years. They had her play small, insignificant roles with just a few lines—a receptionist, a telephone operator, someone's friend. One day they called her into the studio head's office. What she told us, as far as my memory can reconstruct it, was that she got the call at home to be at his office at a specific time. She was nervous, since that was a first. She dressed, put her makeup on, and flew out the door.

"I had no idea what to expect," she said. "I thought that maybe they had found a good role for me to play. I was excited and frightened at the same time. I arrived at the studio, went into the ladies' room to check my makeup, and then went upstairs to the office. The secretary ushered me into a room filled with cigar smoke and the smell of alcohol. Five portly men were sitting around a huge desk in the middle of the room. The head of the studio was behind the desk, chewing on a cigar stub. I was told to sit down, which I did. For what seemed to be a very long time no one said anything. They all looked very serious with their arms resting over their overstuffed bellies. Finally, the head of the studio broke the silence by telling me that they had decided to cancel my contract and let me go. I heard his words as if they were coming from the end of a long tunnel. I was a young actress pursuing a career in Hollywood, and it felt like a death blow. I sat very still for some moments, only seeing the face behind the desk, and then I slowly rose from the chair, looked directly into the eyes of all five men, and said, 'Alright, gentlemen, someday I will come back and buy this studio!'"

Standing erect and to the full limit of her height, she then walked out of that office. She did come back and bought not only that studio but two others!

BEING PREPARED IS NOT JUST FOR BOY SCOUTS

Priscilla Barnes

One of my students, Priscilla Barnes, landed a role in the film *The Crossing Guard,* written and directed by Sean Penn and starring Jack Nicholson, Anjelica Huston, Piper Laurie and David Morse. Sean liked Priscilla for the role, thought she looked right and auditioned her. She played a hooker and in one scene appeared totally topless. Her work in the film was excellent.

On her first day she was tense and insecure, as often happens to actors who come onto a film in midstream. She was working with huge movie stars and felt very obligated to do well. Having trained with me for some time, she had instrumental and craft tools, so she found a spot in a corner of the set, lay down in the fetal position, and did a primal-moan exercise. That technique, which is used to free oneself from tension and emotional blocks, involves making very loud moaning sounds that come from deep in the body. I use it quite frequently in my classes, with incredible results. It is not a preparation exercise that can be done unobtrusively. I am quite sure that everyone on the set heard Priscilla, but I think that her need to liberate herself was stronger than the obvious embarrassment it would cause.

About three or four minutes after she had started, from the other end of the soundstage came a similar loud moaning sound from a male voice. It was Jack Nicholson obviously supporting her. Having spent time in my class, Jack was very well aware of what a primal moan is and why any actor would do it. His involvement was a generous act of support for Priscilla. That is not a surprise to me, though, since he was always encouraging and supportive of me.

CAN I HAVE YOUR AUTOGRAPH?

Steve McQueen

It was lunchtime and I was having a seafood salad at the Old World Restaurant on the Sunset Strip. A couple of tables over from me was Steve McQueen eating something that I couldn't distinguish from my vantage point. He was really enjoying the food and didn't seem involved in the environment. I never intrude on a celebrity under almost any circumstances, so beyond my recognition of him I continued eating my salad. A middle-aged woman with a fifties hairdo and her teenage daughter, who had a ponytail that seemed to move like a metronome when she walked, appeared out of nowhere, scurried up to McQueen's table and asked him for an autograph. He looked up and with what appeared to be a pained expression said, "Please, I'm eating my lunch," at which point they did an about face and sat down at another table. I studied them for a while. Their expressions were easy to read. They looked disappointed and embarrassed at the same time. I was paying the check when McQueen got up, walked over to the mother and daughter's table and said, "If you still want an autograph, I would be happy to give it to you." They smiled and searched for a notebook or something to write on. The mother retrieved a small book from her oversized handbag. McQueen pulled up an empty chair, sat down, asked for the daughter's name, and wrote the autograph. He shook her hand and sauntered out the door of the restaurant.

HOLLYWOOD BEHAVING BADLY

HOLLYWOOD PARASITES

The dictionary definition of a parasite is "an organism which lives, grows, feeds, and takes shelter in or on another organism." Hollywood is full of such organisms! Probably an entire book could be written about this subject. A more digestible way of describing a parasite in human form is to detail the actions of these people.

In 1954 I arrived in Hollywood bright eyed and bushy tailed, ready to start my film-acting career. I came with a friend from college who had the same ambitions. I had one connection with someone that might be of help in establishing me, an actor who had worked with both my brothers at the Jewish People's Institute in Chicago. His name was Joe Mell. Phil had told me how to reach him. He was working as an assistant to a successful agent and was connected to a theater in Hollywood, the Players' Ring, which was the most successful showcase theater around. It was a place where actors in a play could be seen by agents, casting directors and other industry people who could hire them, and it was run by two men, Paul Levitt and Ted Thorpe. I'm not sure whether Ted was an actor, but I knew Paul appeared in small parts in films.

The Players' Ring was an Equity company under a ninety-nine-seat contract, which meant that actors would be paid a salary for their work. Because the seats were limited to fewer than one hundred, that salary was nominal, about fifty dollars a week. That wasn't much, but in 1954 it was enough to pay rent for an apartment and to put gasoline in your car. The more significant reason for getting paid was to boost the morale of the actor, who could then say, "I'm working as an actor and I'm being paid!" Well, it was not to be. Paul and Ted paid the actors, who were then required to return the check immediately if they wanted to continue working there. It was called "kickback"! Because it was such a great opportunity to be seen and possibly to get work, everyone kicked back.

Joe Mell introduced me and my friend Lee to Paul, and we started working immediately as stage managers for a play in rehearsal, *The Rose Tattoo* by Tennessee Williams. And because we were technical staff and were really needed to run the play, Paul and Ted generously gave Lee and me fifteen dollars a week each for our work, which during rehearsals often amounted to ten hours a day. That was in October of 1954, and I worked that show until I was drafted into the army in early January of 1955. After two years in the service, I returned to Hollywood and to the Players' Ring, that time as an actor in *The Cold Wind and the Warm,* and of course all the actors, including me, were still kicking back their salaries. I really don't know how Paul and Ted got away with it for so long, but they did.

There is a line from Shakespeare: "The evil that men do lives after them." In a karmic way nature exacts punishment either in this life or after. While working on a television series in some South American jungle, Paul Levitt contracted a fatal virus that attacked his liver, and he died at a very young age. Ted also left the planet early, and Paul's wife died in a hotel fire in Chicago. Coincidence or retribution?

IS THERE A DEFINITION FOR EVIL?

In my fifty-two years of teaching I have had a large number of incredible experiences. Fortunately, I have a memory like a steel trap that stores everything. I tell people that they should be very careful what they tell me, because I remember everything.

In my early years of teaching I was a partner to Curt Conway, an actor from New York who had been blacklisted during that awful period of the House Un-American Activities Committee. He had come to Hollywood and started teaching. We rented a theater in Hollywood and taught several classes there. (You can read more about that period in my autobiography, *The Diary of a Professional Experiencer.)* Curt had a very attractive woman studying with him, whose husband, Laurence Merrick, had built a theater he had named the Princess Theater. Laurence's real name was Zev Lahavre (or something like that), but he had changed it to Merrick, hoping that he would be aligned with David Merrick, the famous Broadway producer. Laurence was a little below average in height, with black hair that was receding in front and a bald pate at the crown. His eyes were dark brown, which made it difficult to see the pupils, and, wherever he was, they darted around as if searching for something. He leaned forward when he walked, giving the impression that he was stoop shouldered. He spoke English with an Israeli accent and always very rapidly, as if he was afraid of being interrupted or challenged.

Merrick's ambition for success and visibility in the business bordered on psychosis, as he did everything possible to attain his goal. Many of those things were morally and ethically outrageous, and possibly illegal. He had visited Curt's class a number of times and ultimately observed one of mine. From that moment on he was obsessed with wooing me away from Curt and having me teach for himself. He had an office behind his theater, next to which was a little one-room attachment. Since our theater had limited space to work in, I had rented that room to teach private lessons. Merrick approached me almost every day to convince me to leave Curt and come to work with him, although I always told him that I was happy where I was. He even said that he would talk to Curt if I was afraid to do it.

After using the space for a couple of weeks, I noticed that the mirror on the wall that connected to Merrick's office had a section at the top that was separate from the rest. It seemed that a five-inch section had been added at the top of the original mirror. It was obviously a two-way mirror. In fact, if you looked through it closely, you could see into Merrick's office. After inspecting it carefully, I discovered a hidden microphone tucked in behind the glass. Since

I had a list of students scheduled that day, I continued to teach the private lessons. Every time someone entered, I heard Merrick move a chair in his office close to the mirror on the other side. I gave each of my students a little note I had written that cautioned him or her not to reveal anything private in the session, adding that I would explain later. At the end of the day I left in a huff, pounded on the wall of Merrick's office, and walked down the street. He sent his nephew after me to find out what was wrong. I stopped, told his nephew what I had discovered, and indicated that I was going to report it to the police. It was one of the most despicable things I had ever experienced from another human being. I told Curt about the incident, and he laughed, saying that he wasn't surprised at all.

I never encountered Merrick again, but I heard numerous accounts of his actions with other people. He got into making adult movies and somehow claimed the rights as a producer for one he was not responsible for. As happens with evil doers, he was shot by someone while sitting behind his desk in that office. He died on the way to the hospital. I don't know if they ever found out who shot him, but I was told that someone had gone into the dining room of Schwab's Pharmacy (an actor's hangout) and announced that Laurence Merrick had been shot and killed, and that the whole place had erupted in a gigantic cheer. People were on their feet shouting approval of his demise.

THE TYRANT HARRY COHN AND HIS BATTLE WITH RITA HAYWORTH

This story was told to me by my brother Ed Morris, who at the time was still under contract to Columbia Pictures. Harry Cohn was the infamous head of Columbia, and so notorious was his reputation that there are stories, articles and books written about him. In that era the studio heads were all powerful. They could make or break an actor's career with a phone call. As the story goes, one afternoon Cohn and Rita Hayworth were in a pitch battle with each other in Cohn's office. The argument was so heated and so loud that the entire floor Cohn's office occupied heard it. She was screaming at him and he at her, and finally she stormed out of his office and left the building.

Cohn immediately summoned Benno Schneider, the acting coach at Columbia at the time. He told Schneider that he was going to "show that ungrateful bitch that she can be replaced," and he instructed him to bring one of the contract players to his office. He was going to make her a star! Benno suggested a totally unknown blonde, Kim Novak, as the potential replacement. The funny thing about all of this is that just a couple of months prior to that event Cohn had instructed Schneider to drop Kim Novak, telling him that she looked vapid. Schneider now insisted that she had something and that he would like to continue working with her for a while. Cohn acquiesced, and Benno continued to work with her.

Shortly after that, Kim was put into *Pushover,* which was a financial disaster. Her second film, however, *Phffft,* which costarred Jack Lemmon and Judy Holliday, catapulted her to stardom, and from there she did a great number of films, including *The Man with the Golden Arm* with Frank Sinatra; *Bell, Book, and Candle* and *Vertigo* with James Stewart; and a host of others. So Cohn was successful in creating what he thought was his replacement for Rita Hayworth.

On a side note, I knew Kim when her name was Marilyn. We both attended Wright Junior College in Chicago and both appeared in a play at the school, *Our Town.* I played a small role, Simon Stimson the alcoholic choirmaster, while Marilyn had a walk-on as Mrs. Corcoran. Every evening after rehearsal I drove her home. We spoke about many things and laughed a lot. I found her to be a very unassuming girl, who at that time did not express great ambition. A few months later, while we were having lunch in the college cafeteria, she told me that she was modeling at the home show and that she really didn't like being scantily dressed and standing in front of a refrigerator. I lost contact with her after that, since I graduated from Wright and went on to Northwestern University. Years later, after serving in the army and returning to Hollywood to pursue my own career, I wrote her a letter to tell her how happy I was at her success. She responded with a beautiful purple card with her name on it, saying how happy she was to hear from me.

REICHSFÜHRER OTTO PREMINGER

Otto Preminger

Born into a Jewish family, he really wasn't a Nazi; he just behaved like one. Otto Ludwig Preminger was born in Vienna, Austria, December 5, 1905, and died April 23, 1986. He started as a director of plays and later alternated between the stage and films, until his first great movie hit, which was *Laura.* After the success of that film he became one of the top directors in the world and remained so for decades. He was married three times and had two children. The story here, which is based on documentation, rumors and hearsay, concerns why he was nicknamed "Otto the Ogre": He was not a nice man and was at times very abusive to the actors he worked with. He was quoted as saying, "I do not welcome advice from actors. They are here to act!" In the film *Angel Face* he insisted that Robert Mitchum really slap Jean Simmons very hard. When he was filming *Saint Joan,* where Jean Seberg was to be burned at the stake, the wood under her feet caught fire, and to the horror of the people on the set he would not let them extinguish the flames until he had filmed the scene. He was famous for doing things like that, no matter what the consequences might be. At the premiere of *Exodus* the comedian Mort Sahl yelled, "Otto, let my people go." That was a real irony because, as I said before, Preminger was really a Jew himself. In a scene in the same film, while directing several small children, he bellowed, "Cry, you little monsters, cry!" I heard once that someone broke a champagne bottle over his head.

The real tragedy was what happened to Johnny Indrisano as a result of Preminger's insensitivity. Indrisano was a prizefighter, who, as many in the game thought, would have been a world champion in his weight class if he had been handled well. After retiring from the ring, Johnny worked as a technical adviser on a large number of fight movies and also as an actor doing small parts in a variety of films. Directors liked him and would try to keep him working when he wasn't a technical adviser. While doing a small role in a film Preminger was directing, Johnny had some difficulty remembering his lines and Preminger had to retake the scene a number of times. He so badly humiliated Johnny in front of the rest of the cast and crew that Johnny went home and hanged himself. That story has circulated for decades, and I believe it is true. Preminger was a selfish and self-serving human being who could not have had personal happiness. He died at eighty from lung cancer and Alzheimer's disease.

Famous quotes from and about Preminger:

He said, "Directing Marilyn Monroe was like directing Lassie. You needed fourteen takes to get one of them right. Marilyn Monroe, a vacuum with nipples."

Dyan Cannon said, "I don't think he would be capable of directing his little nephew to the bathroom."

THE ANATOMY OF A TALENTED BUT COMPLICATED MAN

Elia Kazan

The following stories involve Elia Kazan and his relationship with others. Three of the stories were told to me directly, and I can vouch for their authenticity. The other two I heard over a period of time, and I believe the sources were dependable. I admire and respect the man for his talent and contribution to the film industry, but I find some of his methods for eliciting performances from actors quite questionable and indicative of deep disrespect for the actors' talent and craft.

MY AIRPORT RENDEZVOUS WITH ELI WALLACH

For a period of three years I traveled back and forth from Los Angeles to New York every other weekend to teach workshops and oversee my theater company, a bicoastal company which we had named the American New Theater. I was the artistic director, and we did plays on both coasts. As a result, I spent a lot of time in airports, as I waited to board my flights.

Eli Wallach

On a couple of occasions I ran into Eli Wallach. Since I knew his background and orientation, I felt comfortable approaching him. I introduced myself and told him that I was teaching and that I too had been influenced by Lee Strasberg. We chatted about the Actors Studio and our respective participation there. He was very open and unassuming, and he seemed to enjoy our conversations. The second time I ran into him I gave him one of my books and told him how much I respected and enjoyed his work. During one of our conversations he related his experience on the set of the film *Baby Doll:* In the scene where he and Karl Malden were running down the stairs of a burning barn, Kazan wanted them to be terrified. He therefore kept them running up and down the stairs until the burning embers were falling around them, narrowly missing their heads. "I'll tell you Eric," Eli Wallach said, "he wanted us to be terrified, and we were!"

That is a perfect example of what Kazan would do to actors to get the reality of the scene. First, it is a blatant disregard for an actor's safety, and secondly, it also shows disrespect for that actor's process and his ability to create the reality. In my opinion as an actor, director and acting coach, Kazan's need to attain the results he wanted did not justify the means.

MIRROR, MIRROR

I was cast in a film by Victor Stoloff, a director who had been visiting my classes for several months. He thought I would be perfect for a suspense thriller he was about to do. I was to play a photographer who photographed what was going on behind a two-way mirror. We rehearsed at the Beverly Wilshire Hotel. The cast included Dana Winter, Albert Salmi and a few other very talented actors. Dana Winter, one of the most beautiful actors in Hollywood, had starred in the original *Invasion of the Body Snatchers.* I already knew Albert Salmi, since he had seen me play Jocko De Paris in the play *End as a Man.* He had been in the original Broadway cast of the same play.

During one of our rehearsals Salmi related a Kazan story to me. He was a character in the film *Wild River* with Montgomery Clift and Lee Remick. Kazan wanted him to be totally exhausted and dripping with sweat, so he told him to run hard for a couple of miles just before they would shoot the scene. Salmi knew how Kazan worked and thought that he could accomplish the same goal without having to run a couple of miles, so he hid behind one of the huge generators and sprayed water all over himself to look as though he had been perspiring profusely. He messed up his clothes, then reported to Kazan, ready to do the scene. Kazan was very happy with the way he looked and how exhausted he was!

AMERICA, AMERICA: *OK, LET ME SEE YOU WALK, HARRY*

I met Harry Davis at the Actors Studio in Hollywood sometime in the seventies. He was a short man with a full head of silver hair, who stooped a little as he walked. His shoulders protruded from his body, and it seemed as if he was being pulled forward from them. He was a New York actor, a longtime member of the Actors Studio, and he had written a one-man play called *People of the Shadows,* which he had performed at the studio in New York. He had also done some parts of it at the Hollywood venue. Having seen it, I felt that it needed a director, so I volunteered to work with him, which he eagerly accepted. I was the head of the directors' unit at the studio at the time, and having seen my work, he was quite excited about my offer. We worked on the project for several weeks before presenting it to the group. Harry said that it was some of his best work, and he thanked me publicly for my contribution to his play. After that we became inseparable. I invited him to my home for dinner. He loved being part of my family. He talked about his life, his career and his marriage in very intimate terms. His wife was a very famous and successful mystery-novel writer, and while he was very proud of her, I sensed that her success eclipsed his own accomplishments and that his self-esteem was critically affected by that. When I was directing him, I worked with him instrumentally and helped him to elevate his self-esteem and sense of entitlement.

One of the stories he related to me was about Kazan: Sometime in 1962 he got a call from Kazan, who wanted to talk to him about the film he had written and was preparing to shoot. It was a sort of autobiography, called *America, America.* Kazan asked Harry to meet him in the lobby of a hotel in the city at exactly twelve noon. Harry was very excited. After all, it was Elia Kazan wanting to see him about a part in his film. Harry awoke that morning at 6:00 A.M., not being able to sleep because of his excitement and anxiety. He busied himself around the apartment, looking for things to fill the time, checking his watch every few minutes. He showered, shaved, and postponed getting dressed too soon for fear of wrinkling his clothes. Finally the time to go arrived, and he hurriedly left the apartment and scurried down the steps to the subway. He got to the hotel ten minutes early and found a comfortable chair, but since he could not sit because of his anxiety, he began to walk through the lobby, circling the entire area numerous times. An hour passed, then two, and finally, when he had resigned himself to the fact that Kazan wasn't going to show up, he left dejectedly and went home. His depression turned to anger and he contemplated calling Kazan several times, until he finally summoned up enough courage to make the call. Kazan answered and Harry asked, "Gadge (Kazan's nickname), why didn't you meet me?"

"I was there!" Kazan answered. "I just wanted to see you walk. You got the part, Harry." It seemed like a typical "Kazanism," but Harry later learned that Kazan had not wanted Harry's walk to come out of self-consciousness. He really wanted to see what emotional life was projected through his body language and gait.

LOSE THE FUCKING GUN

This is probably one of the most famous Kazan stories floating around. It happened while he was filming *On the Waterfront* with Marlon Brando, Eva Marie Saint and Rod Steiger, and it concerns the scene in the car between Brando and Steiger, who was playing Brando's brother, and the famous line Brando uttered, which has been imitated by a generation of actors: "Charlie, I could have been a contender. Instead I'm a bum." In the scene Steiger's character was trying to get Brando to back off and not testify against the syndicate.

At one point Steiger pulled out a gun, upon which Brando said to Kazan, "No! He wouldn't pull a gun on me, Gadge; that isn't right!"

"OK, lose the gun," Kazan responded.

While pretending to hand it to the prop man, he instructed Steiger to pull it out when the scene was actually being filmed—which he did! Brando's reaction was one of those classic moments on film. He responded in the moment. Dropping his head onto his chest, he uttered, "Oh no!" His response was so real and riveting that it has been talked about for generations. So many of Kazan's directorial antics did bear fruit, but, as I said before, sometimes his zeal to achieve reality was a blatant disregard for the actor's talent and craft.

A MEGAPHONE IN THE CROWD

A Face in the Crowd, a film directed by Kazan that starred Andy Griffith, Patricia Neal and Lee Remick, was about a country guy who goes on television as an entertainer and speaks to his audience in a very intimate down-home way. The character was based on Arthur Godfrey, a famous radio talk-show host of the period. Andy Griffith's character goes from being relatively unknown to achieving roaring success. He is not a very good person, and he betrays the very people who put him on top. In one of the last scenes he ends the program and signs off. He is in a booth where he thinks the microphone has been turned off, and he therefore believes that what he is saying on camera will not be heard by the viewing audience. However, Patricia Neal has left the mike on, as a revenge for the fact that he has dumped her for a younger, more beautiful girl he got involved with when he was touring. Everything he says, therefore, is going out over the air. He thinks that the audience only sees him speaking, without sound, but the reality is that they can hear all the terrible things he is saying to them, such as (I am paraphrasing), "Hi, you bunch of morons out there! You don't have a brain in your head. You belong to the throngs of the great unwashed and I hate all of your midget brains." When he realizes that everything he has been saying has been heard by his admiring audience, he is devastated by it. That reaction is what Kazan wanted on film, and to get it he used all of the personal information Andy Griffith had shared with him. At the point where they were filming the scene, he broadcast from the back of the soundstage all of the embarrassing personal things Griffith had shared with him, all of the intimate details of his life Kazan had been pumping him for, and everyone heard it all. Griffith was crestfallen, to say the least! Kazan got what he wanted, and it was real, but at what cost! Griffith was better in that role than he had been before or ever after, which was due to Kazan's directorial manipulation. I don't believe that they ever worked with each other again.

THE BOXING BEAUTICIAN, DENZEL WASHINGTON, AND RUSSELL CROWE

Andre Brooks

A student of mine, André Brooks, had a very interesting experience at a pre-Oscar party with Denzel Washington and Russell Crowe, which I am going to include in his own words. But first, I would like to introduce André. He is a professional Canadian prizefighter, who has had many successful bouts in Canada and here in the United States. He is also a trained hairstylist and beautician, who has cut the hair of several of my other students. He is more than proficient in both professions. He is also a very good actor, who frequently works in films and television.

A while ago he invited me to watch him work out at the boxing gym. I saw him take on the heavy bag and also the speed bag, and I have to say that I had never seen anyone's hands move so fast. His speed was so phenomenal that his hands became a blur. The impact that his fists had on the heavy bag was so powerful that I imagined what being hit that hard would do to a person's face.

Here is the story he told me:

"So, as you already know, back in 2000 I'm at a big Hollywood pre-Oscar party with Brian Bowie (he can confirm all of this) on a Saturday night. I'm walking around well dressed, with a big smile, a strong cocktail in my hand. I'm meeting all sorts of A-list celebrities: Michael Caine, Winona Ryder, Michael Clark Duncan, Diana Ross, Val Kilmer, Ben Affleck, Matt Damon, etc…etc… The host was Ed Lamada (or something like that—Brian can confirm the name). Anyway, then I saw Denzel Washington from across the room, so I went over to congratulate him on his Oscar nomination for *The Hurricane* and to tell him how much I appreciated the fact (that I read) that he had spent a year learning how to really play the part of a boxer. Based on some of the comments I made about his boxing work and the way I was moving as I spoke to him, he could tell I was a fighter. That's when he started asking me more about my background (being a boxing fan himself): how many fights I had, what weight class I competed at, if I ever won the Golden Gloves, what my record was, and so on. Then he asked with a smile, as he nudged me in the ribs, 'So, how many broken noses?'

"I smiled and responded, 'Eight.'

"That's when Russell Crowe said, from about twelve feet across the room, 'Maybe I oughta break it too?'

"Now, remember, this was a conversation in a crowded room between me and Denzel, a crowded room of A-list actors, producers, directors. That was it. Russell had nothing to do with our conversation and was just listening from a distance.

"So…I turned to look in Russell's direction with a smile and quickly realized that he wasn't joking. I gave him a quick stern look and turned back towards Denzel. See, Denzel, a big boxing fan, was very interested in what I had to say. I was enjoying the conversation/stories I was sharing with him, so I wasn't going to let my old bar-brawling habits spoil the moment. Besides, this was America, and I was only a visitor from Canada. I certainly didn't want to be kicked out of the country for fighting. My acting career was only just getting started. So I ignored Russell as best I could to continue answering all the questions Denzel was asking me.

"Then Russell made another smart-ass remark, and I turned to look at him again, but this time I wasn't smiling anymore. I shot him a mean look and made sure he saw that I was pissed. Then I turned back to Denzel to continue chatting, keeping Russell in my eye line.

"Another few minutes passed, and Denzel asked if I had ever fought in Los Angeles.

"So I replied, 'No, I fought in many of the northeastern parts of the United States, such as Detroit, New York, Syracuse, Buffalo, etc…but mostly up in Canada where I'm from.'

"That's when Russell Crowe, again from across the crowded room, said, 'Why don't you go back to Canada?'

"I snapped. I quickly turned and started to walk towards Russell, pointing my index finger as I said, 'Hey why don't you shut your face?'

"The room went completely quiet, and Brian jumped up from the sofa. Russell took a couple of steps back, and just then Denzel jumped between the two of us, holding us apart at arm's length. He said to me, 'Hang on a second, André,' turned to Russell, and started talking some sense to him about who I was, my boxing background, and how important it was for Russell to look his best the next day at the awards show. Remember, he had been nominated for best actor in *The Insider*.

"After a few moments, Russell turned and walked away saying nothing. Denzel then turned to me, put his hand out to shake mine, and said, 'I'd like to apologize for my friend's behavior.'

"To which I replied (with anger), 'Hey, guess what? He may be a great actor, but I'm a great fighter, and if he wants to fucking go, then let's do it!' Denzel, seeing my anger and amped-up energy, placed his hand on my shoulder to calm me down, put his fist out to gesture a brother-type handshake, and said, 'It's cool. Everything is cool.' I gestured back as our fists knocked together, and that was it.

"The important Hollywood people who filled the room slowly returned to their conversations, and everything went back to normal. I quietly wandered off, looking for Russell Crowe on my own. I didn't find him. He had left shortly after the incident. I was pissed and to this day regret not dropping him like a sack of potatoes with a quick left hook, and believe me, I would have. I've knocked out much bigger guys, as well as much more accomplished/skilled fighters than some macho actor. It might have gotten me in trouble, but within a few years of his bad-boy reputation, everyone was tired of Russell and wanted him out of the country. I would have been a hero. It might have really put me on the map much sooner than it has taken me so far. Who knows?

"I'm a fan of Russell Crowe's work and dedication to his craft. He plays the type of roles I'd like to play. I've booked many jobs playing a police officer, but to have played Wendell 'Bud' White in *L.A. Confidential* would have been the ultimate role. I've always looked forward to the day when we cross paths again. In fact, a couple of years later I heard he was training in Canada to play the part of a boxer in the movie *Cinderella Man.* He was actually working out and sparring with many of my old teammates in Toronto. He was also getting his ass kicked on a regular basis, as he was learning the basics of the 'sweet science' (and his opponents were told to 'go easy on the movie star'). If only I had been back in Canada at the time, I would have loved to step into the ring with him and remind him of our altercation…just before the bell rang!"

BS AROUND THE CAMPFIRE

Erik Holland

He had a huge amount of blond hair that rose high above his head. His name was Olav Roger Ovregaard, and I met him in the sixties. Later, he changed his name to Erik Holland and was in a play with me, *End as a Man.* He told me that he had gotten his first professional job from being seen in that show. He came to study with me in my class for quite some time, and we have been close friends ever since. Erik is a really good actor and has done scores of films. I am grateful for his contribution to this book. Here is one of the stories he told me:

"The first day of filming a 'Hatfields and McCoys'-type 'Movie of the Week' up in the mountains north of Simi Valley, we were all sitting around the morning campfire getting to know one another. None of the cast had worked together before, so the producer thought a morning get-together would be nice before we would start shooting.

"Jack Palance almost snuck into our midst, à la Shane, and started shadowboxing really well. I didn't know if he wanted someone to join him or if he was just showing off. There was a rumor that he had broken Marlon Brando's nose when he had understudied

Jack Palance

him in *A Streetcar Named Desire.* Anyway, he started talking about his last movie in England, a horror movie of course. In it was a scene that was supposed to show a child's body burning. Well, special effects couldn't come up with anything realistic enough for the director. Now, while Palance was telling this, he was giggling as if telling a joke. The punch line was that the director underhandedly purchased a child's body from the morgue and had the remains heated so high that the body exploded. Jack's giggling had now turned into raucous laughter, after which the rest of the cast didn't hang out with him much.

"I saw that he was always eating alone, so I joined him. I knew he had been enrolled in the 'sweet science' of boxing. I plopped down, and we chatted on the subject. After lunch we had a scene together, where I, the good McCoy, accused him, the bad Devil Anse Hatfield, of having shot me in the leg years before. I laid on the hostility. He was in front of me, supposedly skinning a deer with a long, sharp knife. I must have gotten to him, because when the director said, 'Cut! Print!' and I went to my dressing room, Jack went to the medic with several cuts on his left hand!"

A VERY TALENTED ARISTOCRATIC ACTOR WITH A CLOSET FULL OF SKELETONS

Franchot Tone came from a very well-to-do East Coast family and gave up working in his father's business to pursue acting. He started his professional career on Broadway in the thirties and was a member of the famed Group Theatre started by Lee Strasberg among others. In fact, Lee named him the best actor in the company, which was quite an honor, since Strasberg was not prone to bestowing compliments on anyone. Soon Hollywood came calling. Tone was under contract to MGM and did a number of films for them during the thirties, forties, fifties and sixties. He was nominated for an Academy Award for his performance in the original

Mutiny on the Bounty, along with Clark Gable and Charles Laughton. Because all three actors had been so good in the film, the following year the Academy established a new category, the "best supporting actor" category. Tone also frequently returned to the stage and, when television became popular, matriculated into that medium.

His personal life was not quite as successful as his professional life. All of his four marriages ended in divorce. His first wife, Joan Crawford, was more popular on the Hollywood scene than he was at the time, so people started to refer to him as Mr. Joan Crawford. He later got involved with, and indeed married, Barbara Payton, an actress who later became a prostitute and was nothing but trouble for him. He was warned by all his friends, including Joan Crawford, to stay clear of her, but he did not heed the warnings and got the hell beat out of him by Tom Neal, another actor who was enamored of her. Neal was an aggressive and violent guy, who had been a boxer in college. Tone had his nose broken and his jaw fractured, and he had a concussion, all of which required surgery. The incident ended Neal's Hollywood career.

Tone wasn't a saint either. He had been kicked out of school earlier in his life for being disruptive and causing problems. A story about him has been circulating in Hollywood for as long as I have been here: While appearing in a play on Broadway, during the break between the matinee performance and the evening show, he wandered across the street to another theater, also on break between matinee and evening performances. He visited with the leading lady of that play, fucked her, impregnated her, and left. I have no idea whether that story is rumor or is in fact the truth. I have heard it from several people over a long period of time, so I am inclined to believe it.

Another story that was circulating around town was that he was somewhat of a voyeur. He liked watching other people have sex. In fact, as the story goes, he hired a very well-hung black actor to have sex with this woman, whom I guess he also paid.

Franchot Tone was a consummate actor. I have always enjoyed watching him work. I just report those stories but make no judgments regarding him.

THE WILD BUNCH

MORE HOLLYWOOD BAD BOYS

There have been many wild boys in Hollywood, dating back to the silent movies. Errol Flynn had sex with an underage girl on his boat and was prosecuted for it. After that, the expression "in like Flynn" circulated in Hollywood for years, possibly decades. It was so popular that many years later James Coburn starred in a film called *In like Flint,* where the main character's name was Flint! Errol Flynn was quite a colorful character. There were rumors that he had been sympathetic to the Nazis, but in fact he was a supporter of the Republicans in the Spanish civil war and a strong opponent of Franco's forces. He was open to trying almost anything for the adventure of it all, including biting the testes off sheep! He was also a very heavy drinker, a habit that ravaged one of the most beautiful faces in Hollywood. He was just fifty years old when he died.

Then there was Tom Neal, who acted in a number of "B" films and a few "A" films—*The Flying Tigers* with John Wayne and a couple of others. His family wanted him to be a lawyer, but he was always taken by the thought of being an actor. While at Northwestern University, he was an outstanding boxer on the boxing team. He debuted on Broadway and later earned a law degree from Harvard. His acting career never took wings, however. He was constantly involved in some kind of scandal or in creating mayhem. He had an on-again-off-again relationship with Barbara Payton, and when Franchot Tone got involved with her, as described earlier, Neal attacked Tone and sent him to the hospital. Blackballed in Hollywood after that fiasco, he turned to landscaping and gardening to earn a living. In 1965 he went on trial for murdering his wife Gale, who had been shot in the back of the head with a .45-caliber bullet. The prosecution sought the death penalty, but the jury convicted him of involuntary manslaughter, for which he was sentenced to ten years in prison. He was released on parole after six years and died eight months later of heart failure. He was fifty-eight years old.

I watched the O.J. Simpson trial on television for weeks and was shocked by the outcome; however, that bad boy was sent to prison for nine years for perpetrating another felonious act. Paul Kelly, a character actor in the forties and fifties, was convicted of murdering a man and spent a number of years in prison. When he was released, he returned to acting and had a moderately successful career. Gig Young killed himself after some kind of altercation with his wife.

AN IMAGINATIVE ACTOR AND A LOOSE CANNON

Timothy Carey

Timothy Carey was a very unusual actor, who had an unusual career to match. He worked in the fifties, sixties, seventies, eighties, and probably until his death in 1994. He attained a cult status playing all kinds of weird, offbeat, psychotic, crazy, or brooding characters, and he was completely unpredictable in his behavior, so much so that many directors were reluctant to work with him, while others liked his willingness to burst out in a scene and improvise, adding lines in an unorthodox way. In *Paths of Glory* the director, Stanley Kubrick, liked what Carey added when he was being executed as one of the French soldiers. Carey, who had no lines in that scene, suddenly blurted, "I don't want to die," and started crying. Kubrick liked it so much that he kept it in the film.

In a scene from *The Wild One* with Marlon Brando, where he played one of the motorcycle guys in the gang, Carey threw a glass of beer in Brando's face. Brando didn't like it, even though he was a Method actor. He did, however, hire Carey later when he was directing *One-Eyed Jacks.* Someone who was on the set of that movie and witnessed the whole thing told me the following story:

Carey was in a scene where he was supposed to throw a bowl of chili at this girl. While doing the scene, he got more and more emotionally out of control, and his behavior escalated to a psychotic fever pitch. The actress in the scene was so frightened that she began to cry. In each successive take they had to clean her up, since she was covered with chili. Her costume, which also had to be cleaned, was damaged so often that they had to keep changing it. They ended up doing more than ten takes without being able to shoot the scene successfully. Brando was livid. After the last take, Carey turned to Brando and, behaving like a small child, asked Brando if he was mad at him. The next day Carey didn't show up on the set, so in order to get the scene they had to put a wig on another actor and shoot him from behind. They finally fired Carey. The irony is that the scene never made it into the film. I'm not surprised, since the first rough cut ran more than eleven hours. Brando never directed another film!

A story about Carey was circulating around Hollywood when I was in my early years as an actor. I don't know how true it was, but considering Carey's antics, it is easy to believe. Even when he wasn't acting, his behavior was to the left of bizarre. He was being considered for a principal role in a major motion picture and was in an interview with the producer, the director, and other members of the producing team. He was looking at the ceiling and listening to their conversation about him and about the character he was to play. The role asked for a very organized, disciplined serial killer. The director looked at Carey, told him how much he admired his work, but added that he didn't think Carey was right for the role, since he didn't come across as a cold killer. At that point Carey stopped looking at the ceiling and made eye contact with the director. He then pulled a revolver out of his jacket pocket, started waving it in the face of everyone in the room, and said, "You don't think I'm a killer, huh? Well, how about I blow your heads off?" Who knew whether or not he was serious? He was Timothy Carey, and anything was possible. Everyone in the room froze. No one moved. Carey stood up and continued his violent intimidation. Someone in the outer office overheard everything and called security. Two very large uniformed men with guns quickly entered the room and escorted Carey off the lot.

HOLLYWOOD'S TALENTED BAD BOY

Dennis Hopper

In 1954 I saw a television show called "The Medic." I believe it was a weekly series. There was an actor playing an epileptic on the show who was brilliant. I thought I caught his name in the credits, Dennis Hopper. He was so compelling that I never forgot it. As the years went by, he did a number of films and was in *Rebel without a Cause* with James Dean, whom he idolized. I'd say he was a bad boy, but actually he was more like a loose cannon. He was into drugs and was doing crazy things. I read in a magazine that he hung out with a lot of young actors at the time, including Natalie Wood. One evening, thinking that it would be great fun, they filled a bathtub with champagne and put a naked Natalie in the tub. It burned her vagina so badly that she screamed and leapt out.

Flashback: I got out of the army at the end of 1956 and was on an audition right off Sunset Boulevard on a side street right near the Cock 'n Bull Restaurant, a Hollywood landmark where a lot of celebrities used to hang out. It no longer exists, just like so many of the other famous Hollywood clubs that have disappeared, such as Earl Carroll's, the Brown Derby, the Coconut Grove, Ciro's, and so on. I was walking to where I had parked my car, and there was Dennis, wearing a cowboy hat, boots, and a Western-style shirt, wielding a nine-foot bullwhip, whipping the shit out of a white Ford Fairlane and screaming obscenities at the car. I stopped and looked at him, and when he turned and saw me, he smiled and said, "That fuckin' car is the biggest piece of shit in the world and I'm going to kill it!" He stopped and smiled again. I don't remember what my reaction was, but I do remember that I walked on. I didn't know Dennis at that point. I met him a number of years later through some of the people I hung out with. Maybe it was Jack Nicholson I met him with. He did a number of films and was always very good in everything he did. He was in and out of drugs most of the time. When he did *Apocalypse Now,* he was so stoned that he actually passed out during one of the takes. That film was fraught with problems. Martin Sheen supposedly had a heart attack during the filming and there were issues with Brando. Coppola certainly had his hands full.

In his later years Dennis straightened out and gave up most of his bad habits. He had a scene in *True Romance* with Christopher Walken that was incredible, so memorable that it stood out as one of those unforgettable movie scenes. Dennis started painting, and I understand from everything I have heard that he was a very good artist. It isn't always the case, but so many very gifted people are also very troubled.

NOT SO EASY RIDER

Stories and rumor are swirling around the making, the casting and all the trials involved in filming *Easy Rider,* which was released in June of 1969. Dennis Hopper and Peter Fonda came up with the story of two "countercultural guys riding colorful motorcycles from Los Angeles to New Orleans, looking for America." The story I had heard was that they ran the idea by a producer at Columbia, who gave them four hundred thousand dollars and told them that it was all he would allow them and that they had to bring the picture in for that.

It was the sixties and drugs were a big part of the coming of age of the youth of America. Haight Ashbury in San Francisco was a hotbed of all kinds of hallucinogens. The aroma of marijuana filled the air like cheap perfume in a barber shop. The music of the period and the lyrics resonated with the mantras of the drug culture, and if you were young, you were cautioned not to trust anybody over thirty. That was the atmosphere that prevailed around the making of that film.

Dennis Hopper, the director, was a young actor who was about to give up acting and become a teacher—or so the story goes—so when it became possible for him to direct that film, he jumped at the opportunity. In those days he was pretty stoned much of the time.

Rip Torn was originally cast in the part that Jack Nicholson later played, but in a preproduction meeting Dennis pulled a knife on Torn in an altercation, and that was the end of Torn's participation in the project. Bruce Dern was offered the role, but he turned it down because of a schedule problem in relation to another film. Another actor was also considered, but that never materialized either. The day before they were to shoot the scene where Nicholson's character first appears, they still did not have an actor for the part. Because the budget was so small and they already had the location, they could not afford to waste the time or the space. Hopper suggested Jack for the role, and they ran a script over to his house the night before he started on the film—or so that story goes. It was also rumored that in the scene where all three of the characters get stoned on grass, the actors were really smoking it. It was definitely a memorable scene.

During the film two of the motorcycles used in it were stolen, and they had to make serious adjustments to some of the scenes. A great number of crew members quit because of Hopper's drug-induced rages. Hopper used many of the people who lived in the area where the film was shot.

While the film was in postproduction, I ran into Jack at the Plush Pup, an outdoor restaurant on Sunset Boulevard, and he told me that he was editing his own scenes. I deduced that it was because they had run out of money at that juncture. I asked him about the film and how he felt about his work, since he and I almost always found a way to talk about acting, and as I remember, he was pretty positive about what he had done in the film. It is said that when Henry Fonda saw the movie he said that if Jack didn't win an Academy Award for his performance he would quit the business. *Easy Rider* was voted number 84 in the best one hundred films of all time.

THE AGE OF NEFARIOUS

Jimmy Davidson

The following story was told to me by a dear old friend, James Davidson, whom I have known for at least forty years. I ran into him at our health club and told him about this book chronicling the experiences and relationships I have collected over the last half century. Jimmy is an actor, who in fact took my class sometime in the late sixties. He said that he had an interesting story to tell. He related it to me, and I asked him if he would be willing to put it on paper and give it to me, since I thought it would be more than just an interesting "Hollywood story." Here is what he wrote:

"You know how it is when you think back on an incident and how you might have changed the circumstances or altered some invidious jerk's physical appearance or just made yourself feel better by standing tall in the face of an impending shit storm? Well, that moment, emblazoned in my memory, took place at a time when the confluence of forces, better known as 'the sixties,' presaged an idyllic era…the promise of good will for all…the emergence of the flower child…the era of the love-in.

"Pursuing the lifestyle of the fledgling actor in always-balmy L.A. in 1968, I was lucky enough to work in the last days of TV westerns. I lived in the ideal place to indulge all of my passions. I had discovered a ramshackle cottage, really a converted tack room, in one of the narrow canyons leading into Will Rogers Park—a perfect place to have horses, dogs, motorcycles and cars. If you stood on the roof of my house at sunset, you could glimpse the Pacific through the shaggy eucalyptus trees. The legend of my little shack was that it had once been among the favorite trysting grounds for Errol Flynn. Could it get any better?

"On my way to work early one morning, I had thirty minutes to make a 6:00 A.M. call in the Valley—a trip that, with no traffic, took forty-five minutes. I was entering the hilly section on Sunset near Will Rogers at a good clip, when I noticed another Speedster tailing me. I digress here for a moment to mention that one of my aforementioned passions was finally owning a 1955 Porsche Speedster. And, as all Speedster pilots know, the sweeping curves on Sunset spiraling in from Pacific Coast Highway are the perfect testing grounds for your tolerance of centrifugal forces or your attitudinal adjustment in traffic court. Back to the race: In a flash, the gleaming black Speedster was by me, launching into the curve on a perfect line. The snarling downshift rap from the exhaust evidenced that this guy knew what he was doing. Needless to say, the duel was on! I took the lead back as we emerged at the top of the hill leading onto the straight shot through the Rivera, only to notice too late that we had just been nailed by the motorcycle cop sitting back on Amalfi. Patiently enduring a lecture from the gendarme, my recognizably famous racing partner and I lucked out with a warning. We laughingly shook hands on our good fortune; and, after we had compared notes on our cars, he went home from an all-night crawl, and I went to work. That's how I met Dennis Wilson, who was one of the founding members of the Beach Boys.

"We ran into each other again a few weeks later. As it turned out, we were both patrons of Stan's, a health-food lunch counter/hangout at the wrong end of Cañon in Beverly Hills. In those days the famous and near famous gathered to partake of the fad of organic sticks and seeds offered by Big Stan, along with his philosophical pronouncements thrown in as a side dish. The topics ranged from the importance of Reichian therapy and the Orgone Box to driving fast and telling outstanding lies. On that rare-for-L.A. rainy afternoon, Dennis tumbled in through the shop's backdoor with a gaggle of scruffy-looking hippie chicks and this dwarfish guy in a jumpsuit—only to be met with Stan's instantaneous opprobrium. Apparently, Dennis had given his Rolls Royce to the group to use as a troopship; and they had previously been seen dumpster diving and camping out in the alley behind Stan's store, much to the consternation of his neighboring shopkeepers. The ensuing harangue between Jumpsuit Guy and the physically imposing Stan soon descended into a volatile debate on 'the man' vs. 'the unwashed,' that ended with the banishment of the gypsy troop from the premises. Stan suffered no fools.

"Dennis watched them leave in amusement, commenting to Stan that they were just another bizarre aspect of the music business and that he was helping them out by introducing them to the right people. *Noblesse oblige* was perhaps the guiding dictum operating here, but it seemed Dennis was inordinately generous, which, as I got to know him better, was accurate.

"In a rambling conversation that same afternoon, we determined that we both lived in the same canyon, albeit at opposite ends. Dennis lived in the Uplifters Ranch area with its one-of-a-kind architectural log cabins, put together as a bohemian gathering spot by the friends of Will Rogers in the early 1900s. My little 'ranchette' straddled the same canyon several miles back in the meanderings of the riverbed, which allowed for hiking or riding unimpeded to State Beach. We both vowed to ride that trail someday, as I had access to horses stabled at Will Rogers polo grounds.

"Over the following weeks, our friendship seemed to thrive on all things mechanical, such as adjusting a carburetor on one of the cars or getting the correct Avon tires for a Triumph Bonneville at Bud Elkins' shop in the Valley. Our common bond was a shared passion for fast bikes and cars, particularly Speedsters. The artistic endeavor is so ephemeral that having a tangible construct such as building an engine for a bike or restoring an old barn was gratifying and necessary for real world equilibrium, at least for me. We never articulated that thesis, but we did discuss the foibles and blandishments piled up on the pop artist in the music industry. I recognize with the advantage of hindsight that his meteoric rise to fame as one of the vaunted few in the world of music didn't sit that well with him, which gives me an insight on his acceptance of all who crossed his path. 'Uneasy lies the head that wears a crown,' I reckon.

"Sometime that summer, I was invited to a dinner given by Dennis for his record-industry friends at his nifty cabin in the woods. The house was reminiscent of Teton Lodge, surrounded by redwood trees, with a parking area littered with Ferraris—a mythical scene. I attended with my date, who enjoyed the attention of the assembled music honchos, as it was unique compared to her New York theatrical background. During dinner, which was presided over by someone I remember as 'Calvin,' a movie-star-handsome, majordomo-bodyguard type who seemed to look after Dennis, we all settled into a raucous exchange of stories around the table, mostly centering on the picaresque adventures of Dennis the

Menace, as he was known to his friends. The semi-esoteric barbs flying back and forth generated that sense that you were witness to a rarified climate shared only by the anointed princes of the record business, or maybe a lesser Algonquin Table.

"There was a palpable pressure drop in the room and a hardening of Calvin's demeanor when a new bunch of people drifted in from the dark. I recognized them as the same gypsy gang banished from Stan's earlier in the year. Dennis welcomed them to share dessert, and they intermingled with the guests as the banter resumed. Several of the guests, including my date, clamored around the new arrivals to hear the musings from the lower depths. I got absorbed in conversation with a lyricist who sometimes collaborated with the Beach Boys, and I wasn't paying attention when I clearly heard the words, 'Fucking Nigger.' It stopped the room cold. The defamer was none other than the scrawny guy in the jumpsuit referring to Calvin, who could have easily dismantled the offending idiot. With admirable insouciance, Calvin dismissed him as an 'ex-con who'd had a bad time in juvie,' and continued on, unabashed.

"The coven coalesced around their leader, who, knowing he had been punked, stepped up his vituperative diatribe with equal opportunity insults to all, who, incredulously, seemed to crave his abuse. Maybe the manifestation of the so-called radical chic of the era explained their indifference. I, however, took umbrage at a comment from the little jerk made to my date concerning her privileged Jewish background, and I entered the fray.

"I think I said something to the effect that, although Calvin was duty-bound to maintain decorum, I had no such compunction and would gladly modify his outlook. Out of the corner of my eye I caught the disapprobation of the guests and the glint of fierce challenge from the brood standing in battle formation. Jumpsuit, having backed away from his humiliating challenge with Calvin, now had to deal with me. Bad voodoo! This is that fraction of a second when you evaluate punching the guy in the mouth or letting it slide and not destroying the evening. Hell, I didn't really know any of those people—I hardly knew Dennis—and they all seemed to court the alchemy of danger posed by the association with this 'bad guy' as part of their higher understanding. This, added to the fact that I hadn't been in a fistfight since my high-school days in a foundry town, presented me with the archetypical Hamlet conundrum. Screw it! I resolved to drive my fist through his smirking mouth, when he blinked. He scurried away and threw out some face-saving comment about my having a silver spoon up my rear end. It was over. The creep resumed his poisonous rant; and as absurd as it sounds, many of the guests stood in rapt attention in an amazing display of appeasement. I was now the turd in the Kool-Aid. This was not a place I needed to be at. I didn't like those people. With sycophantic approvals of the miniature minister's bullshit echoing in the background, I gathered up my somewhat embarrassed date and left. I never saw Dennis Wilson again.

"On that terrible August night a year later when the news of the Sharon Tate murders paralyzed Los Angeles, we all felt the overwhelming loss of the feeling that we were safe in the world. Some months later, when it was revealed that Charles Manson and his minions had committed this wanton act of butchery as part of some maladroit philosophy borne out of his distorted view of world order, I finally put a name to the face and thought back to when I had been witness to his evil evangelizing. Eastern philosophers postulate that each individual act alters the course of future events in a salutary fashion. Therefore, had I done something different that night at the party, could it have changed things? Probably not."

HOLLYWOOD TRAGEDIES

Over the years there have been numerous fatalities involving Hollywood personalities. Since the forties and even earlier, there have been suicides, plane crashes, murders, disappearances, and so on. Carole Landis, a movie star in the forties, was found dead on her living-room floor, apparently a suicide. Carole Lombard, who was married to Clark Gable, was killed in a plane crash while on a bond-selling tour. Inger Stevens was also a suicide. Natalie Wood, Marilyn Monroe, Elvis Presley, Heath Ledger, Whitney Houston, and many others met with a tragic death. For some unexplainable reason I have been somehow connected to several of those people who were involved in horrendous happenings. Most of the stories I am going to tell involve me in a direct or indirect way. I knew many of the people and was indirectly involved with others.

SHARON TATE AND THE MANSON MURDERS ON CIELO DRIVE

That terrible night when all those people were killed by some of the members of the Manson family rocked all of Los Angeles. In the same week the Labiancas were murdered in a similar way. It was 1969, and just a few months earlier I had spent an hour coaching Sharon Tate for a movie she was to appear in. The following is the story of my experience with her and the tremendous impact it had on me:

Sharon Tate

One afternoon I received a call from Sharon. I knew who she was, having seen her in a few films. She asked me if I could give her a private lesson. She was preparing to do a film and needed some help. She told me that Jack Nicholson had recommended me and that she needed to see me soon. When she walked into the theater, standing in the doorway with the light framing her from behind, she looked like a saint in a religious icon from the Middle Ages. As she came into the room, it was as if she radiated her own light. She was startlingly beautiful. She told me that she was having trouble being terrified and that it was an important obligation in one of the scenes in the film. I asked her what frightened her, but she had a difficult time coming up with any real fears large enough to address the scene. I suggested a number of possibilities, which I frankly don't remember over forty years later. At any rate, none of my suggestions worked. I finally told her she was beautiful and had the face of an angel, and I asked how she would feel if someone cut her face to pieces.

At this point I must say that for all these years, in light of the events that followed in that poor woman's life, I have regretted what happened next. I told her that I had a very sharp knife in my pocket and that I was going to disfigure her for life. I put my hand in my pocket, where there was no knife, and began to advance towards her. Her face went white, all the blood drained from her head, and she started to scream with the most terrifying terror I had ever seen. I quickly removed my hand from my pocket, threw both hands in the air and embraced her, whispering into her ear that I would never hurt her and that I had just been exploring a choice she might use for the film. She calmed down but held on to me for several minutes. When she broke the embrace, she smiled at me with gratitude and affection and said that she now knew what to do. On the way out she turned and said that I had not been oversold and that she would be back to work with me. That was the last I ever saw of her. A while after that encounter, I heard the news about her death and was very sad. Besides being physically beautiful, she was also beautiful inside, very soft-spoken and warm. I think she was probably in the early stages of pregnancy but hadn't yet begun to show.

It is a strange feeling to have known some of the people who were murdered that night. I also knew Jay Sebring, who had a tremendous reputation as hairstylist to the stars. We had met at the Factory, a very trendy disco in Hollywood, and had had a number of conversations about his ex-wife, Cami, who was in my class and had talked to me about him. He was in the house the night the Manson gang broke in and killed all the people.

In addition to Sharon Tate and Jay Sebring, I also knew the house Roman Polanski and Sharon were renting. Located on Cielo Drive, it was quite secluded and mostly off by itself. The owner, Rudy Altabelli, was in Europe at the time. Rudy, an actors' manager, handled a number of my students and came around to the class occasionally. He was quite successful managing big name actors and had a few whom he felt he could usher to stardom.

During the week of the Tate-Labianca murders Los Angeles was the tensest city in the United States. Everyone was on edge and frightened. It was before the Manson family was apprehended, and everyone was looking over his or her shoulder. It was a hot July afternoon. The Circle Theater, where I conducted my classes, didn't have air conditioning, or maybe it just wasn't working that day, so I had opened the doors to the outside to get a little air into the place. The entire class was lying on the floor doing a relaxation exercise, while I was sitting in my usual chair. Suddenly, out of the corner of my left eye I saw a black-and-white pass on the street. I thought nothing of it until moments later, when two police officers coming in from opposite directions, guns drawn, entered the room and stopped in their tracks as everyone on the ground sat bolt upright. The officer who had come in from the front door lowered his pistol and said, "Well, you must admit that it looked very strange from out on the street." Both policemen were embarrassed, but that is exactly the way it was in our town that week.

ANOTHER HOLLYWOOD TRAGEDY: PEOPLE I KNEW

It is one thing to hear about a celebrity's death and quite another when you have known that person.

Stirling Silliphant

Sometime in the late seventies I was coaching a student for an audition. It was a very good role in a miniseries called "Pearl," a story about the events leading up to, and including, the attack on Pearl Harbor. My student, Tiana, was the wife of Stirling Silliphant, a major Hollywood screenwriter, who was also the writer for the miniseries. It was a very demanding role, in which she had to have a complete emotional breakdown. For most actors, to be able to reach that emotional level on cue, particularly in an audition, is quite daunting. We worked for a week, several hours at a time, and finally, with my coaching Tiana was able to reach the obligated goal. She auditioned and got the part. I was invited to go to Hawaii to continue to coach her on the film. My wife Joy and I were flown first class to the island and put up in one of the best hotels in Waikiki.

Natalie Wood

It was there that I met Robert Wagner and Natalie Wood. Wagner had a role in the film and Natalie was there to be with him. The Silliphants, the Wagners, my wife and I met at a restaurant on the beach and talked all afternoon. I found Robert Wagner to be very down-to-earth and one of the nicest people I had ever met. Natalie was very quiet and seemed shy. She spoke little but seemed quite involved in the conversations. Stirling was very gracious and also direct and easy to relate to. Tiana was quiet, although I could feel her excitement at being there and doing the part. Natalie took to Joy and through her hairdresser asked her to go shopping with the two of them. As it turned out, Joy was busy with me at the time and couldn't go with the two women. Robert also seemed to like Joy and had many conversations with her while we were on the set.

The second time I ran into Robert and Natalie was on the island of Catalina. The Wagners and I had boats in the same marina at Marina Del Rey, and quite often I would pass their boat, the *Splendour,* as I was heading out to the ocean. One of the places people with motorboats visit is Catalina. I saw them approaching us there. With a huge smile Robert said, "Well, Eric, we must stop meeting on islands." We laughed and spoke for a few minutes. Natalie again was quiet but quite friendly. Joy and Natalie strongly resembled each other. They were both small brunettes, and they shared an emotional quality that was very similar.

I am not sure how long after that Natalie drowned in the ocean near where the *Splendour* was anchored. As reported in the newspapers and on television, her death was ruled an accident. That night Robert, Natalie and Christopher Walken were on the boat. They had been drinking, and an argument broke out between Robert and Natalie. As reported, it was fairly violent emotionally, and Natalie stormed off and seemingly disappeared. Robert called her and searched the boat, but she was nowhere to be found. The theory was that she had jumped into the dinghy and moved away from the boat, but because she had been drinking, she had fallen into the water and drowned. The next morning they found her body floating a fair distance from the *Splendour.* She was in her early forties. It was truly a Hollywood tragedy.

A TRAGEDY THAT DID NOT HAVE TO HAPPEN

I met Brandon Lee in New York when I was teaching there every other weekend. He came to several of my workshops while attending Emerson College. We worked together for many months, and he finally came to my Los Angeles classes and studied with me for over a year. While he was in my class, he got his first starring role, playing David Carradine's son in "Kung Fu, the Movie" on television. He had to shave his head, which he did gladly. We threw a big party at my house to celebrate his booking of the part. I thought that Brandon was quite talented and hoped that he would avoid following in his father's footsteps. When I was teaching in Manila, I saw a billboard the size of a building advertising Brandon in one of his first films. It said in big bold letters, "Starring the son of Bruce Lee." When I returned to Los Angeles, I had a talk with Brandon. I told him about the billboard and cautioned him not to create a career in the shadow of his famous father. I had seen Brandon do some martial-arts moves at a weekend workshop at my house in Lake Arrowhead, and while he was proficient, he was nowhere near as good as his father.

Brandon Lee

After some time had passed, he drifted away from class and did another movie. I ran into him and we spoke briefly about the direction he was going in. He told me that he didn't want to be "another Bruce Lee," in spite of the fact that he adored his father, but that if it was the key to the door of success, he was going to open that door. I understood but didn't agree with his decision. I told him that he was a very good actor and could do many kinds of roles other than physical ones. He agreed with me but felt that Hollywood was a hard nut to crack and that he was going to take advantage of any opportunity that presented itself. Shortly after that, he got the role in *The Crow,* and the rest is tragic history.

I heard about his death hours before it was announced. My ex-wife Joy had a former student working for a national news organization. She called me in tears to tell me that Brandon was dead. He was twenty-eight years old and was to be married to Eliza Hutton on April 17. I am including a description of the circumstances of the accident that caused his death as reported in his biography from IMDb, the International Movie Database: "Brandon died on the set of *The Crow* (1994). The film crew shot a scene in which it was decided to use a gun without consent from the weapons coordinator, who had been sent home early that night. They handed Michael Massee the gun loaded with full power blanks and shot the scene, unaware a bullet head from an inert round had accidentally been lodged in the barrel. Even though the gun was pointed away from Lee, the force from the blank curved the flight of the bullet head and it shattered his spinal cord. The crew only noticed when Lee was slow getting up. The doctors worked desperately for five hours, but it was no use. After his spinal cord was shattered, he had no chance of survival. He was pronounced dead at 1:04 P.M. the next day."

I have a lot of trouble accepting that story. First of all, how did the head of a bullet get into a revolver in the first place? Secondly, since when does a bullet travel in an arc like that around corners? Nonsense! I am an actor with over one hundred films under my belt, and I have been on enough sets to know that live ammunition is never allowed on any set anywhere! I am also a gun collector and know almost as much about guns as I do about acting. Even with a full loaded blank, the energy of the blank being able to propel a lodged bullet with enough force to do the damage they say it did is questionable. The blank would have been separated from the projectile by several inches from the bullet head, and when fired, the energy of the blank would dissipate a great deal of its thrust in the barrel and most likely would have discharged the projectile but without the power that is generated by a bullet. I suspect there was a great deal of misinformation about the whole event. The original story that I heard is that the film was being shot on location and that the film company had hired a less-than-professional crew. Instead of buying blank ammunition, which it is possible that they could not locate, they bought real .44 Magnum bullets, pried off the head of each bullet, and stuffed wads in each of the cartridges. The theory is that one of those bullets escaped the attention of the prop people and remained a live round, which was accidentally put into the gun that killed Brandon, and I believe that that gun was definitely pointed directly at him. At any rate, Brandon is dead and I am sure that it was a tragic accident, but I still have the theory that I just shared.

THE LIFE AND DEATH OF FRANK WOLFF, ACTOR

I met Frank in 1959 at the Players' Ring Theatre in Hollywood. We were both appearing in *The Cold Wind and the Warm*. I was a character love struck by Barbara Landau, and I believe Frank

Frank Wolff

played my older brother. We became friends, and he encouraged me to go to Martin Landau's acting class. I had met Marty during the run of the play, since he would appear every night at intermission to visit his wife, Barbara. Frank and I were in Marty's class for a couple of years. He was a big guy, not so much physically—although his height was greater than average, he was well built and you might even refer to him as stocky—but because of his compelling personality and his affable smile. It was impossible to dislike him. He worked as an actor in Hollywood, did a number of Roger Corman films and landed an important role in *America, America,* written and directed by Kazan. It was in Europe that he became a star, however, working for legendary directors, such as Sergio Leone and other important European directors. He appeared in a number of spaghetti westerns, and when that trend died out, he did a number of Italian crime movies. I had even heard that he was warned not to do one of those movies by the Mob and that he replied, "Nobody tells me what to act in!" As many actors know, there are a lot of disappointments in an acting career, and I am sure Frank experienced his share of those disappointments. He lost to Ringo Starr a role that he had really wanted and that had been promised to him in a film called *Blindman.*

Sadly, Frank killed himself in the Hilton Hotel in Rome in December 1971. He was forty-three years old. It was a commonly held theory that he had suffered from depression and had felt that his career was at an end and that he couldn't get the roles he truly wanted anymore. There was another rumor floating around about his suicide, however: He had killed himself in the bathtub of that hotel room by amputating his testicles and cutting his throat because he was suffering from the impact of being rejected by a woman he was in love with. I heard that from a couple of sources, but I don't know if there is any truth to it.

On a personal note, I loved Frank. If it hadn't been for him, my life would not have taken the direction it did. He was responsible for guiding me on a path that led to my success as an acting teacher, a career that has occupied the largest portion of my life.

THE BOY WITH A SPARKLE IN HIS EYES

Bobby Driscoll

It was 1957 or '58 when I met him. His name was Bobby Driscoll, and he was in a play that I was stage-managing at the Players' Ring on Santa Monica Boulevard in Hollywood. Driscoll was one of those actors who grew up in the industry and were schooled by teachers brought to the set of whatever movie they were working on. As a child actor, he had done a Disney feature called *Song of the South,* as well as a number of other films. In *The Window* he had played a small boy who witnesses a murder while looking out his window. The killer sees him and begins to stalk him. In 1953, being under contract to Disney, he had done the voice of Peter Pan in the animated feature. He was one of the most critically acclaimed child actors and at the age of twelve had won a special Academy Award as the outstanding juvenile actor of 1949 for his incredible work in *So Dear to My Heart* and *The Window.* Bobby's expression and the sparkle in his eyes were very much like those of a small child sitting by the Christmas tree who has just opened the most desired present in his life. He always looked as if he had been injected at birth with the joy of living.

The play I was managing was *Girls of Summer* and also starred Michael Connors—before his success in television series such as "Mannix"—and Carole Mathews. Bobby and I became friends. At every intermission, his friends would visit him backstage: Bobby Blake and Dean Stockwell had both been child actors and were still actively involved in films. I was invited to sit in on their conclave. The conversation was quite interesting and sometimes a little shocking. Here were three child actors I had seen in films over the years, grown-up and talking about their sexual activities. It was a little disorienting, since I still saw them as grown children. I started to look forward to those intermission meetings, which became the highlight of doing the play.

Bobby had been a very popular child actor, but as he grew older he developed a serious case of acne and the studio dropped him. After that it was difficult for him to find work. He did a few plays in Hollywood and then went to New York looking for work. He got into drugs and his life plummeted. On March 30, 1968, his body was discovered in an abandoned Greenwich Village tenement by a couple of children who were playing there. At the time, his identity was unknown, and since his body was never claimed, he was buried as a John Doe in a pauper's grave at Hart Island, a potters' field. A year later his fingerprints revealed his identity.

Bobby was a special person with talent and a lust for life, another casualty of the Hollywood machine.

HE ATE DOG FOOD AND SOLD ROLLS ROYCES

All Hollywood tragedies are not about famous people. This is a story about one of the many thousands of actors who are pursuing a career in Hollywood. Becoming a movie star is the great fantasy that ensnares young people to journey to Hollywood, seeking fame and fortune; but too many of them give up the journey only to return from where they came, frustrated, disillusioned and depressed by their lack of success.

I knew him from around town. I had seen him numerous times, never on an audition but in places where actors congregate. He was tall, with a full head of light brown hair, a rosy complexion, and a killer smile. His name was Shawn McNamara. He had an Irish name obviously, but not a particularly Irish face. I would sit next to him at the counter at Schwab's and listen to his stories, which were interestingly boring. He was in his early thirties at the time. He was an actor, but I am not sure that he had ever had a paying acting job. He was making a living selling toner to businesses over the phone. He knew that I was an acting teacher, and on various occasions he would ask me questions about what I taught. I knew that he was interested but wasn't ready to make a commitment to training. I didn't push it, and as a matter of fact I was extremely cool about creating an opening for him to jump into.

One day at the counter he finally said, "You know, I think I would like to come to your class for a couple of months and brush up on my acting." I didn't let him see what I was thinking, which was that I knew that in a couple of months I couldn't teach him how to spell his name! He came and stayed for seven years!

Shawn was one of those characters that you never forget, possibly because they are so quirky, bizarre, and unpredictable. He collected guitars, had twenty of them, and he played and sang at every weekend workshop he attended. He had a modicum of talent but not the kind that could translate into making money at it. He lived in Santa Monica and his guitars took up his entire garage. He had done numerous jobs to support himself, even on one occasion selling Rolls Royces in Beverly Hills. He was so broke that he wasn't able to put food on his table. He had two dogs, chows, which he loved, and he made sure that they would not go hungry. He woke up each morning, took a shower and dressed meticulously in a clean white shirt, a nice suit and a beautiful tie. He sat down at his kitchen table, ate a whole can of dog food and left for work. That was all before I met him. At that juncture he was selling products over the phone and running down to pick up the cash from the company he was working for. He would alternate between moments of depression and humor.

He did many scenes in my class and became a competent actor. He would always tell me that the class did as much for his personal life as for his acting, and he was grateful for that. I liked him a lot. He made me laugh and I enjoyed his humorous sarcasm, which always seemed to be directed towards himself.

On New Year's Day 1995 I received a phone call from a mutual friend of ours telling me that Shawn was dead. He had died New Year's Eve. I was so shocked by hearing that that my legs buckled under me and I fell back on my bed. Not being able to speak, I listened to my friend telling me what had happened and how Shawn had died. It seems that he was returning from Vancouver, having visited his brother over the holidays and having had a terrible fight with him, which had come to physical blows. He had left and gone to San Francisco to go on an acid trip with a guy and a group he had been involved with before. As a side note here, he had been asking me to accompany him on one of those acid trips, telling me that the insights and discoveries were mind boggling and that with my talent and perception the potential of great discoveries and breakthroughs were guaranteed. My response was always the same: I told him that I was high on life and that I was completely drug free and would remain that way. At a house in San Francisco, Elliot (not his real name), the leader of that glorious trip to be experienced, was surrounded by about ten other people. During the "trip" Shawn became angry and so violent that they had to subdue him. They duct taped him to a bed. His entire body was bound by the tape, with his arms and legs close to his body in mummy fashion. Everyone went to sleep thinking that Shawn would be all right in the morning. During the night he swallowed his tongue, was unable to rescue himself and choked to death. He was forty-one years old at the time. That was seventeen years ago, and to this day I see him through my mind's eye and hear his infectious laugh. I miss him.

LEIF ERICKSON (NOT THE VIKING)

Leif Erickson

He was an actor—kind of big. He worked with Kazan a couple of times, the first time in the play *Tea and Sympathy* and a year later in the movie *On the Waterfront,* where he had a small part. Kazan had an uncanny eye for seeing people's personalities, their weaknesses, and their character traits and flaws. Erickson was a man's man and macho to boot. I think Kazan somehow suspected that all of that macho bravado was somehow covering something well hidden beneath the surface. The role Erickson played in *Tea and Sympathy* was perfect for him: As the housemaster in a school for boys, he liked spending more time with the boys on camping trips than with his wife, and he felt only disgust for the main character, who was very sensitive and suspected of being gay.

Erickson's son Chris came and studied with me sometime in the late sixties or early seventies. Linda Cristal, who was in "The High Chaparral" with Leif, had sent Chris to me. He had been in Vietnam as a Green Beret, a Special Forces unit that was usually selected to do very dangerous jobs. He had volunteered for that unit and was a fiercely aggressive soldier. He told me several horror stories about that war and his specific experiences, which seemed to mirror an action-adventure movie. In one of the stories he was in a helicopter circling above a hill on top of which one of his Special Forces soldiers was marooned, while a company of Vietcong soldiers were making their way there. It was certain that his friend would be killed, since there were more than forty of the enemy coming up that hill. Chris pleaded with the helicopter pilot to drop him next to his buddy so he could help him, but the pilot refused. He knew it would be certain death for both of them. Chris understood what the odds were and insisted anyway, but to no avail. Of course his friend was killed.

That kind of blind heroism had been instilled in Chris from childhood by his father. He told me that Leif would sneak up on him and punch him in the stomach, and when he would double over in pain, crying, Erickson would reprimand him and tell him to "be a man." Leif would also systematically challenge him to do dangerous things, make him run up and down hills until he would fall exhausted, and brainwash him with stories of how cowards live and the humiliation they undergo constantly. It seemed that to die heroically was better than living the shameful life of a coward.

Chris didn't die in Vietnam. He died in a car accident, driving a Volkswagen van on Pacific Coast Highway. Because of his history, his end seemed to be the fulfillment of a death wish.

HOGAN WASN'T A HERO

A number of years ago among my acting gigs were several appearances on the television series "Hogan's Heroes." I played a variety of roles, mostly German soldiers and officers, and I had a scene or two with Bob Crane, who played Hogan. I experienced him as being aloof and arrogant. He would always disappear right after doing a scene. He never hung around with the rest of the cast. A typical Hollywood actor, he wore his military hat pushed back on his head, so we could see his hair and he could look cool. From our first encounter I sensed something inauthentic about him. His smile would immediately disappear when the director said, "Cut!"

I can't help thinking that if we had had colonels like him in the army during World War II, we would have lost the war!

I also got to know Richard Dawson, one of the regulars on the show, with whom I spent many hours between takes talking about politics, the movie industry and acting. He was a very personable and informed guy.

Bob Crane

A number of years later, after the series had become part of television history, I heard that Bob Crane had been found dead in an apartment in Scottsdale, Arizona, on June 29, 1978. It was assumed that he had been murdered. Since I had worked with him and knew a little about his career, I followed whatever information I could find. "Hogan's Heroes" had been the pinnacle of a somewhat disappointing career. In his early years Crane had been a disc jockey on radio. He had started acting when he was thirty-three and had appeared on numerous television shows, such as "The Love Boat," "Quincy M.E.," "The Doris Day Show," and several others. "Hogan's Heroes" lasted for several years and accumulated one hundred and sixty-eight episodes. After it ended, Crane had his own television show, "The Bob Crane Show," which was a failure and only ran for fourteen weeks. He then began doing dinner theater, capitalizing on what was left of his television fame.

The real story about "Hogan," alias Bob Crane, was that he was a voyeuristic sexaholic, who would lure women to his apartment after each show, ply them with drugs, and have them perform various sex acts with each other and I assume with him and his friend John Carpenter, while they filmed all the action with two cameras. He would use the women, and when he was finished or sexually satiated, he would give them to Carpenter.

Crane was found dead in his bed, bludgeoned with an object that they couldn't find at the scene. Recently I had the pleasure of speaking to Rod Englert, a crime-scene reconstructionist who was brought into the case ten to fifteen years after the murder. I asked Mr. Englert why it had taken so many years for them to reopen the case, and he told me that at the time there hadn't been enough evidence to go forward. Even though Carpenter was the suspect, it wasn't until they started using DNA as evidence that they arrested and tried him for the murder. The prosecution determined that Crane and Carpenter must have gotten into a horrific argument, which had escalated into the violence that followed. Carpenter was angry because Crane didn't share the most attractive women with him. In a sense he felt he was getting the leftovers. Englert testified for the prosecution, but Carpenter was acquitted, because the DNA they had found in his car could not be used as creditable evidence, since there was too little of it and time had seriously degraded its value.

On the bed sheet where the body was found was a bloody imprint, which they thought might have been made by the murder weapon, but it was difficult to establish what object had made it. They hadn't found the weapon that had killed Crane, even though they were careful to examine the room very thoroughly. It was assumed that if they could identify the object that had made that imprint, they might be able to tie it to Carpenter. So the prosecution decided to explore. They went to a high school in the area, and without telling the students what they were doing, they used a variety of objects, including a camera tripod, to make imprints on a fabric that resembled a bed sheet. As it turned out, the tripod made a perfect imprint on the sheet, exactly like the one they had found at the scene of the murder. Mr. Englert told me that four months after the murder, I imagine while looking at the crime-scene photos, they had noticed that one of the cameras was on the floor while the other one was on a tripod. Why they hadn't figured out at that time that the tripod was the murder weapon is somewhat of a mystery. Still, they couldn't tie it to Carpenter, so he was acquitted in 1994. He died in 1998.

Several ironies were connected with Crane. One of them was that the play he was doing in Scottsdale was titled *Beginner's Luck.* There was also a rumor that he was virtually broke at the time of his death. The irony is that shortly after his murder the series was sold into syndication and would have netted him millions, since he owned a piece of it. He was buried in a cemetery in Chatsworth, but his widow later moved him to the prestigious Westwood Cemetery on Glendon Avenue, a place where many movie stars are interred.

GUNFIGHT AT THE ANIMAL CORRAL

I saw a movie once where one of the characters was telling another that a young man reads the comics in the daily newspaper but when you get old you read the obituaries, and so it is with me. Today, while perusing the *Los Angeles Times,* I was very saddened by reading that Pat Derby had died of throat cancer at the age of seventy. I knew Pat. She was a special person, a lover of animals, to which she dedicated her entire life.

Pat started studying with me in the mid-sixties. At the time her name was Pat Shelley. She was born in Sussex, England, and was related to the famous English poet Percy Bysshe Shelley. Besides having a love affair with all kinds of animals, she expressed an interest in acting and attended my class for many months. During that time she met another animal trainer and got married. Ted Derby was a handsome guy, with black curly hair and a smile that lit up a room. Pat was a small, very attractive brunette with a personality that radiated warmth and love. In fact, she once told me that relating to or training animals was all done with love. Animals know when you love them, and they respond in kind.

Ted and Pat continued to attend my classes until they moved up to the San Francisco area, at which time they would fly or drive down to Los Angeles to take private lessons with me. I was then renting a small house on Highland Avenue, where I was teaching my group classes as well as private lessons. I remember it was a warm sunny day and I had an appointment with Pat at 1:00 P.M. at that house for a lesson. I climbed the three steps to the front door, and when I opened it, there stood a five-and-a-half foot bear on his hind legs, who was quickly approaching me. I freaked, screamed and flattened myself against the wall. Pat yelled that it was OK. "He is very friendly," she said; "he won't hurt you!" By the time the bear reached me my heart was racing at warp speed. He put his paws on my shoulders and began sucking on my chin. "You see," Pat said, "he likes you!" After a short moment that seemed like eternity she called him off. He found a corner in the room and lay down. She told me that he was a sun bear. The yellow area on his chest was how he got the name.

Both Ted and Pat worked with animals of all kinds—tigers, bears, wolves, dogs—and trained them for the movies. Pat worked on "Flipper," "Gunsmoke," and "Lassie," as well as on a variety of films where animals were involved. During that time the Derbys' involvement and success in the industry took them away from their pursuit of acting, but they kept in touch with me, giving me updates on their involvements. Pat became disenchanted with the way the studios were treating the animals, and she quit to become one of the most powerful animal activists in the world. She formed an organization, the Performing Animals Welfare Society (PAWS). She was a giant of the animals' rights movement and would go head to head with anyone she felt was mistreating an animal, including the Walt Disney Company. She had many nicknames, such as "The Elephant Lady," or "Tiger Woman," and she even wrote a book called *The Lady and Her Tiger.* She was once quoted as saying that the Hollywood chapter of the American Humane Association, which certifies films using animals, was little more than a public-relations firm for movie studios. She nursed animals that were sick and dying back to health and could encourage them to do any kind of trick or behave in any way she wanted them to. She was an unsung hero. One time I asked her if she was ever afraid that an animal would attack her, and she told me that she had no fear, because no matter how much of a wild animal it was she knew that her love reassured it and that animals only attack a trainer if they are mistreated or feel unsafe or threatened.

The obituary said that Pat had separated from Ted because he wanted to use an electrical prod on an animal and she would not tolerate that kind of cruelty. That, however, is not true. The real story is that they had an animal compound somewhere near San Francisco or Sacramento and Ted had a violent disagreement with a neighbor, I imagine over the animals and the compound. The two met in an open field and faced each other as in the Old West: They drew their pistols and had a gunfight in which Ted was killed, shot to death. I know this to be the truth, because Pat called me to tell me about Ted's death. She was crushed by it. That was the last time I heard from her. I read that in 1976, while working with her cougar in a Lincoln Mercury ad, she met Ed Stewart and they were married. At her death they had been together for thirty-seven years.

HE SURVIVED *THE GODFATHER*, BUT NOT A NEW YORK CITY BUS

Richard Bright

Richard Bright was a friend of mine. He, his actress wife, Rutania, and I met regularly at the Source restaurant on the Sunset Strip. We would sit at that outdoor restaurant for hours sometimes, discussing acting and the business. Richard was a regularly employed character actor, who had done a lot of work in New York and Hollywood. He was in *The Godfather* saga and appeared on major television shows. I lost contact with both him and his wife when they moved to New York. I spoke to Rutania a couple of times and sent her my autobiography, which she enjoyed and spoke to me about after reading it. The next thing I heard was that Richard had been killed by a tour bus while crossing a New York street. He had been run over by the rear wheels of the bus. The driver didn't even know about it until the police tracked him down at the bus terminal. Richard had a son with Rutania and will be missed.

IT IS A TRAGEDY IF YOUR CAREER DIES BEFORE YOU DO

Hubert Cornfield was a film director, as well as a student and friend of mine. He had an early directing career in Hollywood that essentially started in 1955 and ended in the late sixties. One of his first films was *Lure of the Swamp,* a "B" picture. His second feature, *Sudden Danger,* was followed in the same year, 1957, with *Plunder Road.* His work in those films attracted the attention of some of the cinema magazines of that period, who regarded him as a very talented and innovative film maker. He began the sixties with *Angel Baby,* but his breakthrough film was *Pressure Point* with Bobby Darin and Sidney Poitier in 1962. Having difficulty finding work after his last film, *Night of the Following Day,* starring Marlon Brando, Richard Boone and Rita Moreno, he moved to France and there directed his last film, *Les Grands Moyens,* in 1976. All in all Hubert directed a total of seven films.

As I recall, Hubert came to my class in the late sixties, and he was very taken with my work and the system that I teach. He was there as a director, but as he wanted to experience what actors deal with, he acted in several scenes in class. He was quite believable. He also directed scenes, and his critiques were insightful and perceptive. We lost track of each other for some years, and when we reconnected he had been through a major bout with esophageal cancer. The surgery had taken a large part of the right side of his face, his jaw, and his vocal chords. He was seriously maimed and very self-conscious about his appearance. When a person loses his vocal chords, he cannot speak, so a device that is held to the throat transmits the voice, which sounds rather like a science-fiction transmitter and is very irritating to listen to. Hubert rejected it and with painstaking effort learned to speak by forming the words in his mouth using his lips and tongue. At first it was hard to distinguish what he was saying, but very soon, if you really listened to him, you could understand everything. I was amazed at his accomplishment and thought that if he wanted to he could teach others to do the same. I remember that Sanford Meisner also lost his voice to cancer and did use that device to communicate.

To me Hubert was one of those special people who might have changed the world in some definitive way, and it is hard to understand why his career ended so abruptly. Many artists ruin themselves by being difficult, egocentric and just a nightmare to deal with. That was not the case with Hubert. It seemed to me that everyone liked and respected him and even when he criticized an actor's work, he did it in a very benevolent way. At one point in his journey through life he was homeless, and he lived for a while in his van. At night he would find deserted parking lots that he could use. That was a time when we were not in contact. I learned of his plight later, when some benefactor helped him to rent an apartment. I visited him at that time of reconnection. He had written a screenplay, involving the Nazi period and the Holocaust, which was so rich in characters that once you started reading it you couldn't put it down. He sent the script to Gregory Peck, whom he had known at an earlier time, thinking that Peck might somehow get involved in the project. Mr. Peck wrote him a beautiful letter, which

I read, saying that it was a wonderful project that must be made into a film for the people of the world to see, but that because of his advanced age and his decreasing energy he could not participate in it. He added, however, that he wished Hubert great success and that he respected him.

The last time I saw Hubert was in a health-food restaurant on La Brea Avenue. He had seen the interview with Johnny Depp on "Inside the Actors Studio" where Johnny spoke about me in very complimentary terms. He called me and asked me to meet him for lunch. After just a few minutes I understood the reason for our meeting: Hubert thought that because Johnny Depp had so much respect for me, I might be directing one of his films, and he felt he could back me up and work on a project like that. I could see his desperation and his need to grab onto something that might get him back in the saddle. I was very kind to him. I really liked and respected him and was not about to do anything to hurt him. I explained that my relationship with Johnny Depp consisted in my having spent three days in a Baltimore hotel room with him, coaching him for one of his first films, *Cry Baby,* and that he had also come to my house in Hollywood once for a private lesson when he was about to do *Edward Scissorhands.* His interview on "Inside the Actors Studio" was in relation to what he had gotten from my books. "When I read *No Acting Please* by Eric Morris," he said then, "it put it all together for me." When Lipton asked him whom he credited with his acting training, Johnny responded by saying, "Stanislavski, Strasberg and Eric Morris." I purposely reiterated all of that to Hubert so that I could communicate to him that my relationship to Johnny Depp was not one where I would be called on to direct him in a film. Hubert died shortly thereafter.

I have been acting and teaching for over half a century in Hollywood, and I consider myself one of the lucky ones. I am a successful teacher and have a blessed life, but Hollywood chews up and spits out legions of people who come here to realize a dream and are often shattered by the insensitivity of our industry.

THE COST OF SEEKING FAME

Joi Lansing

She was beautiful and sexy and had an endearing smile. She looked a lot like Marilyn Monroe and had competed with her for a couple of movie roles, which Marilyn landed. Her name was Joi Lansing, and she died of breast cancer. With a body that rose above a number ten, she had a large, full and appetizing bust. In order to fulfill the slot of sexpot she had her breasts enlarged by silicone implants, which ultimately leaked into her system and killed her.

Joi was in my class in the early sixties. Besides her incredible good looks, she, like Marilyn, had a disarming childlike quality. She was a "party girl" and got involved with a large group of famous actors, such as George Raft, Mickey Rooney and Frank Sinatra. Married four times, she was obsessed with stardom and seemed to be able to do most anything to achieve it. She started out modeling when she was quite young and because of her good looks ended up on the silver screen, at first in very small roles, some of which were uncredited. She appeared in a couple dozen films and in 1955 began acting on television, on shows such as "I Love Lucy." When she finally landed a running role on "The Bob Cummings Show," she was at last regarded as someone who could act. From there she went into "The Beverly Hillbillies" as Lester Flatt's wife. Both those shows ran for several years, and she finally began to taste real success and respect, only to die at the age of forty-three.

Another student of mine, who unfortunately did not achieve visibility in the business, also died of breast cancer because of silicone implants. It took a while, but the use of silicone was finally outlawed.

THE TRAGIC LIFE OF BRIAN KELLY

Brian Kelly

Brian Kelly was an actor in Hollywood in the sixties and seventies, who appeared in many episodic television shows, such as "The Beverly Hillbillies," "Adventures in Paradise," and numerous others. His breakthrough role was on "Flipper," a series about dolphins where he played the leading character. Even though he always felt that he took a backseat to the dolphins, that series made his career.

The story of Brian Kelly was told to me by Hampton Fancher, a very close friend of mine and of Brian's. Hampton and I go back to the early sixties when he joined my class. He was an actor—and a very good one—who had done a lot of TV and a host of films. For whatever reason, he stopped acting and became a writer. He wrote *Blade Runner, The Mighty Quinn,* starring Denzel Washington, and also wrote and directed *Minus Man,* starring Owen Wilson. At the moment he is writing a sequel to *Blade Runner.* I will talk more about Hampton later in the book.

I asked him to tell me Brian's story firsthand, since he was there when a tragic accident ruined the life of that well-known, successful actor. Here is what he said:

"Brian was an irresistible human being in every way. One of the finest people in the world, he could just go to the store to buy a pack of cigarettes, and when he finished telling you that story you would be lying on the floor laughing. He could also laugh at himself. Born in Michigan, where his father was twice governor, he was a privileged guy, and he was kind of arrogant, but at the same time so self-effacing and humorous that people really liked him anyway. He was so handsome that women would walk into walls when they turned around to look at him. He just had this irresistible animal magnetism and was full of humor and sexuality. He seemed simple and yet honest and sophisticated, and he had a small-town quality about him. He was impressed by Hollywood and was kind of the king of Miami for a while, because he had that television series, 'Flipper,' but he was embarrassed about that and made fun of it. Nothing was funnier than to listen to him talk about the porpoise, of which there were a few. He directed some of the episodes, and so he came out of it with a high 'TV-Q,' or whatever they call it, and was kind of in demand in a way.

"Brian had been in the marines at the end of the Korean War. He was a man's man, and it was hard to imagine him being afraid of anything. One night we were driving down the street and we got into an altercation with another car on Sunset with about six college guys. They screamed, 'Pull over, motherfucker,' so we all jumped out of the car, and I thought we were going to be killed, but Brian just lifted his hands, saying, 'They are registered,' and just by the way he said it they backed away. He seemed like a guy who could never be a coward, never, never. He would land on his feet no matter what happened.

"And then he got this film. It was a huge attainment for him, because everyone in Hollywood wanted the part. The movie, called *The Love Machine,* was based on one of the biggest-selling books that year and was supposed to make Brian a star. Both the studio and his agency were totally behind it. Brian was on the Johnny Carson show and was being wined and dined, but inwardly he was scared to death. He was really nervous and challenged to finally headline a movie, which at that point looked as if it was going to be the biggest film of the year. As I said, other stars were trying to lobby to get that part, but Brian got it. I think he had to test for it.

"Then he asked me to help coach him through it, which was unheard of, because he had never talked about being insecure about acting. He didn't take it seriously; he was an athletic guy, while acting was kind of a hobby; and yet he was secretly impressed with the idea of stardom and was intimidated and anxious, although I can say I didn't know that then. He asked me to help him and said he would pay me, but I said, 'No, no, we're friends.' We had been to Europe together a few times, and we lived the high life. We pulled practical jokes on each other. I followed him through Europe once for three months, not knowing where he was. I was supposed to meet him in Berlin, in London, in Nice, in Rome and literally more places than that, but I would get to the hotel or wherever it was, and there would be a message that he had just left. He would play pranks like that. I was doing an interview in Munich in a hotel suite I was living at, sitting at a table on the terrace of my own private suite, while three or four people from the press were talking to me. One of them was taking pictures. Suddenly a full can of garbage fell on me from above, off the roof. I was covered in garbage. I knew who it was. We did things like that to each other. He was a fearless cutup, a guy who would pretend not to laugh when he thought something was funny. He always had to be on top, and he was. He was charming and I loved him. I was flattered that he liked me.

"So he had just come back from Europe, had just gotten *The Love Machine* to star in, when I realized—as we'd go in these dunes up in Northern Malibu and would sit in the sand, and I would question him about the role and about himself—that the reason he was very laissez-faire about acting was that he was really intimidated to admit that he didn't know anything, that he felt ignorant. There was a whole part of him that was in the closet, so to speak. He wasn't the kind of guy who could apologize or could say I'm really frightened, or I don't know what the hell I'm doing, where do I start or what do you think is a good idea. So I was quietly trying to help him, and I could see he wasn't getting anywhere. He was distracted. Before Thanksgiving, just after Sharon Tate, I think, and all that—'72, '71, I am not sure—he had shot some tests for the film. They wanted to do some costume and hair tests, so he shot those. They found them later during the trial that followed. I could tell then that he was really nervous.

"On Thanksgiving Day I was supposed to go to his house for dinner with a lot of people—Gary Lockwood and various others who were actors and in the business. It was a beautiful November day, God's perfect day. At the time, Bryan was living with his girlfriend up in the hills in Benedict Canyon—or maybe on Beverly Glen before they built all that stuff—while I lived in Laurel Canyon. I had two motorcycles then, a Honda and a Triumph, and I borrowed another one anyway. I had a friend take one of them up to the house, and I drove the other with my daughter. I got to the house and came in, happy to see Brian. He seemed nervous and quieter than usual, more subdued, more inward, though he was not an introspective person. Days before he was to start shooting, he had become very quiet, and I didn't know till later that it was really fear. He was challenged by something. He always thought very highly of himself, and people treated him very well, as if he were kingly in a way—which he was—and he hadn't admitted to himself that he was frightened of acting and that he didn't know what he was doing really; but it had caught up with him, I think, and that's why he had become very quiet.

"In the back of my head I was thinking that it was such a beautiful, sparkling day I thought it would be great to take a ride. Brian was such an athletic guy and had told me so many stories about his vehicle prowess—his race-car driving, airplane flying, motorcycle riding—that I never thought anything but that he was really good on a bike; and so, as he was cooking and whistling, while his friends were arriving, I kept on telling him, 'Come on, man, let's take a ride up on Mulholland. I brought the other bike, and you got to see this day. You can see for many miles, and it has never been more beautiful,' but he didn't respond to that, and it bothered me. 'Come on, man,' I repeated, 'it will take ten minutes,' but again he ignored the request. Three of us were there, all very close friends at the time. I got the other guy, a lawyer, on the other bike, even though he didn't know how to ride, and we went up the hill. He almost killed himself, and it was fun! Then we went back down to the house, and he said to Brian, 'Man, it is so incredible you got to go up with Hampton.' I too encouraged him, and finally he said, 'OK, OK,' and he got on the Honda, the slower of the two bikes. I knew that he had not been on a bike since Miami, but what I think is the real story is that he had never been on a bike. He just told those stories because he was a wonderful storyteller. I must have told him some bike-racing stories where I had wrecked myself, so he told some too.

"I lived with my daughter then, who was thirteen. I thought it would be fun to take the girls with us, so I took my daughter on the back of my bike, and Brian took my nanny on the back of his. He went before me on this little access road, and I remember he was really awkward on the bike and didn't look right. The nanny was holding him around the waist, and we arrived at the access to the road at the same time; but my friend the lawyer and his wife were leaving in their car, so I parked for a few moments to say good-bye to them, while Brian went up the hill towards Mulholland. There was no traffic, nothing; it was perfect. He went off slowly, and I thought it was funny that he didn't gun it to take off, you know. He just went put-put-put. I said some more things to my friend the lawyer, and then I turned left to follow Brian, who was just a little ahead of me. I could hear his motorcycle, but I couldn't see him because he had turned a corner.

"When I went around the corner thirty seconds later, I saw my nanny running towards me on the road, kind of hysterical and waving her arms. There hadn't even been enough time for Brian to have revved up the bike. He was slow falling off, it seemed, because he was lying on the other side of the road, while the bike was partly on the curb. We had put each other on so much, however, that I thought it was a put-on and that he had put the nanny up to this hysterical behavior. She was running back towards me yelling, 'Someone, help!' but she wasn't hurt, and so my daughter and I walked up to Brian, joking and fucking around. I thought that maybe he was fooling the nanny too and had just fallen over. I kicked him a little with my foot on his shoulder and back, and right then I saw there was some blood on the side of his head where he had fallen. He had hit his head just lightly, because there was only a drop of blood. That freaked me. I knew he was passed out, but he seemed OK, except he was unconscious. I bent down to try to revive him, and then I saw that he was starting to turn gray. He went into shock, and I didn't act very well. I didn't know what to do. I should have gotten his feet higher than his body. Instead, I stood up, stricken and kind of hysterical. I put my hand over my mouth and said, 'Oh God, oh God!' I knew he was dying. Just then somebody stopped, a Good Samaritan, an old guy who knew the score and who said, 'Help me pull the bike over. Have something to put his feet up on high.' So we pulled the bike over and propped his feet up, and the color returned to his face; but he was obviously out, so someone in the neighborhood called an ambulance.

"I remember the feel of his hand. There was no traffic, so I sat there on the street holding his hand, and I was sad, but I knew that he was going to be all right. He was breathing OK, just unconscious. When the ambulance got there, I remember getting into it and asking, 'Where are you taking him?' to which they replied, 'UCLA.' I followed them, thinking, He will be conscious again; he's fine, because his head looked good; it was just a little scratch, basically, from gravel or something.

"Hours went by, and then the news came: he was in a coma, and they would have to do CT scans and all that stuff. It was devastating, but I said to them, 'Well, it's Thursday, and he has got to shoot on Monday. I mean he's got to be good for Monday, right?'

"He wasn't good for a long time. They had to recast the film. He was in a coma for a month, and when he came out he had brain damage. He was basically a gimp. His right arm and right leg were useless; he had aphasia and couldn't speak right. He lost his masculinity, he thought, because he wasn't the man he had been; he wasn't the beautiful guy, he wasn't the movie star; but he adjusted to it. His arrogance and his superiority, which were always fun—heroic more than a pain in the ass—held him in good stead, you know. He lived his life without self-pity. It took him a year to reconstitute and be able to talk again, and he never talked properly. I was with him a lot. I found him a new place to live, and I was involved in his physical therapy. I would show up.

"If it hadn't been for me, it wouldn't have happened. I never felt horribly guilty, because it seemed so much of it was serendipity. OK, I was an asshole. If I hadn't pressed him, he wouldn't have taken that ride, but I didn't think he couldn't ride. Still, I have always felt terrible and responsible; I feel guilty about many things, but I never felt complicit in his demise, except just mechanically. I was very close to him in those first couple of years when he was reconstituting himself, especially in the first month. I was always impressed with his aplomb, that he could do all this—try to learn to walk, to talk. A couple of therapists were involved. He used to go to therapy, and I would drive him, until finally the therapists started coming to his house.

"Another sad thing is that he and his girlfriend had been breaking up before the accident. In fact, he had been staying in a hotel the last few days as an excuse for preparing for the film; but actually he was having an affair, she was having an affair, and they weren't in love with each other anymore; but he had lost his memory of that last month or so, and so she was stuck staying with him. It took time to break up, and he thought—he never got over the idea—that she had left him because he was no longer the man he had been; so it was very sad, but he acted brave about it all, as if it were water off a duck's back. He had a maid who stayed with him and lived in his house. She made his food and cut it, because he couldn't use but one hand.

"One winter day, after leaving his house following a therapy session, I doubled back and peered through the window to see him alone. He was sitting on the couch as if watching television, but the television wasn't on. He was sitting there crying, though he never cried, not even in the worst of shit.

"Another time we were sitting together just relaxing and he asked me in his distorted speech, 'Do you believe in God?' He never used to talk like that. He was not a philosophical guy. So I said, 'No, I don't.'

"'So you never prayed?' And I thought that he would only say something like that as a joke; but now it wasn't a joke, and it was very touching.

"He died about six years ago. He did get married after the accident, and his daughter was taking care of him. There was a settlement after the trial, a court proceeding about a glitch in the motorcycle—which he won—and so there was money. He died of some kind of cancer. I think he was in his early seventies."

GOD CRIES EVERY TIME A PARENT LOSES A CHILD

I was speaking to Jack Nicholson on the phone shortly after my son passed away, and he told me that Francis Ford Coppola too had lost his son.

I met Francis Ford Coppola sometime in the sixties. He came to my class and observed the work but never made any comments. After several months, he came to where I was sitting while teaching, thanked me for what he had gotten from the class and told me that he would not be coming back. His first picture was for Roger Corman, and the rest is history. He is one of our greatest film directors and writers, having won many awards for directing, producing, and writing. In 1986 he lost his son, who was killed in a boating accident while Francis was directing a film in Washington, D.C. My heart goes out to him. We share the grief of having lost a child, which never leaves you. Our children continue to be in our lives every day.

STIRLING SILLIPHANT'S TRAGIC EXPERIENCE

Stirling Silliphant had sixty-five titles to his credit, including *In the Heat of the Night* (for which he won an Academy Award), *The Towering Inferno, The Poseidon Adventure, The Grass Harp,* and a slew of others. As a result of working with his wife, as described above, I became friends with him, and he and Tiana even came to one of my weekend workshops in the mountains. He reluctantly participated, even though he wasn't an actor. He had been married a number of times before Tiana and was older than she. The tragedy that he experienced was that his son was shot to death. Apparently his son had gone to the front door to respond to the doorbell, and when he opened the door, he was shot. I don't know whether they ever found out who killed him.

ANOTHER FATHER LOSING A CHILD

One evening before my class had started, a young man walked into the room. He was attractive and well built, with a shock of reddish blond hair and a smile that was immediately ingratiating. "Hi," he said, "I would like to sit in on your class. I've heard great things about you and I would like to study with you." I shook his hand and invited him to take a seat. His name was Dean Paul Martin. He was the son of Dean Martin. I immediately liked him. He was courteous and respectful. He observed the work and seemed genuinely impressed with what he saw. After the class was over, we spoke for quite some time, but he never mentioned that Dean Martin was his father. He shook my hand and told me that he was definitely coming back to join the class. It was strange watching him leave the room. I had a very peculiar feeling that I would never see him again in spite of his enthusiasm. Not too long after that, I heard that he had flown his jetfighter into the side of a mountain and had been killed. He was a pilot on a training mission for the Air National Guard.

Dean Martin in his last years was quoted as saying, "I would give everything I have to spend just one hour with my son." I can relate and agree with that totally.

WHERE WAS THE BABYSITTER?

I guess if you live long enough, tragedy finds you. I have known Bruce Dern for around fifty years. He directed me in the play *End as a Man*, or at least in most of the rehearsals. At the time of their tragedy, his wife was Diane Ladd, also a very fine actor. They had gone out for the evening, leaving their small boy in the care of a babysitter. When they returned home, they found their child dead in their swimming pool. I am not sure what had happened. I am only reporting what I heard. Here again is a tragedy that is so devastating that it colors the rest of your life. I ran into Bruce recently at a restaurant, and he was very warm and supportive of my career.

THE TRAGEDY OF LOSING A SPOUSE

William Shattner lost his wife. I heard that she had drowned in their pool. Our paths crossed a couple of times many years ago, once at a party given by an actress he and I had dated at different times, and again at lunch at the studio where he was doing "Star Trek." He is a very nice man, and I was saddened when I heard of his wife's death.

The same thing happened to another friend of mine, Nathaniel Brandon, a famous psychologist, who was involved with Ayn Rand. She had dedicated the first edition of *Atlas Shrugged* to him. Nathan had sent his wife, Patricia, to study with me. She was an actress, and he felt that she could benefit by being exposed to the way I worked. She was in my class for a while. One day, when Nathan returned home, he discovered her floating face down in their swimming pool. She had apparently suffered an epileptic seizure, had fallen into the pool and drowned. There is no way to understand why bad things happen to good people.

FOOD CAN BE LETHAL

A number of years ago I was in a private session with Coleen Lanza, the daughter of Mario Lanza, the great tenor and movie actor. She had come to me because she was interested in pursuing

Mario Lanza

an acting career. I worked with her a few times and thought that, besides being quite attractive, she seemed to have some talent too. I told her how much I admired her father's voice and that I had seen almost all of his films. I thought he was a fantastic opera singer, who could have competed with people like Caruso. He did in fact play Caruso in the movie *The Great Caruso*. She told me that he had eaten himself to death! He was so into eating that it had taken over his whole life and he had become almost obese. It had affected his career, as he had been replaced by slimmer actors. I lost touch with Coleen, but, as fate would have it, at my fifty-year high-school reunion in Chicago I ran into a classmate who was Lanza's wife's sister. She told me that a few years earlier Coleen had been run down by a car and killed, as she crossed a Chicago street. Mario Lanza's wife also died shortly after he did.

MANY FATAL ACCIDENTS HAPPEN IN THE HOME

Jeff Corey

An actor and acting teacher, Jeff Corey had achieved a great reputation as a character actor. He had done dozens of movies and was the most recognizable acting teacher in Hollywood when I started to pursue my career in 1957. He was the one go-to teacher at the time. Jack Nicholson had studied with Jeff, who kind of adopted him. I never did train with him, since my brother Ed arranged for me to be in another class. Over the years and after I started to teach, Jeff and I had a number of telephone conversations about acting, and in 1980, as I mentioned earlier, we were both in *Battle beyond the Stars*. We had several scenes together, and I really enjoyed working with him. He fell in his home, suffered a fatal injury, and died. I had last seen him at the AFI award ceremony for Jack Nicholson, and he looked great! It was not long after that that he died.

Jeffrey Hunter also died from an accident that occurred in his home. He fell off a ladder and apparently hit his head and died from the injury. It is very strange that so many of these people have somehow crossed my path, directly or indirectly. Jeff, whose real name was Henry (Hank) McKinnies, was a student at Northwestern University in the theater department. We had the same acting teachers and the very same educational background. He graduated in 1949, and I in 1954. We had a chance meeting at the Players' Ring Theatre in 1957, where we spoke for almost an hour comparing experiences at NU. We had both been taught by the infamous Alvina Krause, who had a theater in the summer in Eagles Mere, Pennsylvania. Jeff had done a season there, but when I had asked her if I could go, she had turned me down. Her claim to fame was that she had worked with actors who later became famous, such as Jeffrey Hunter, Charlton Heston, Ann-Margret, Patricia Neal, and a few others. Jeff had a very good career, which floundered in later years, as happens to many actors. He was strikingly good-looking and had bright blue eyes—which was kind of strange when he played Jesus.

Another actor who died in his home, one I didn't personally know, was Frank Silvera. He was a black actor who, because of his light skin, played many Mexicans, Native Americans and so on. Frank was electrocuted while fixing some kind of fixture in his home. He too had done some teaching in Hollywood and, with an African-American actress, had formed a theater company called The Theater of Being.

WAS HE INTOXICATED OR NOT?

William Holden died from a fall in his own house. He slipped on a throw rug, hit his head on the corner of a coffee table and bled

William Holden

to death. His body wasn't discovered for almost a week. There was some controversy about whether he had been drunk or not, but as far as is known that was never proved. Holden was a huge movie star, appearing in dozens of films. His first Hollywood role was in *Golden Boy* from the play by Clifford Odets. He also appeared in a number of Hollywood blockbusters, such as *The Bridge on the River Kwai, Sunset Boulevard, The Wild Bunch, Network* and scores of other films.

IF YOU HAVE A PORSCHE, BE CAREFUL DRIVING IT!

James Dean

It was September 30, 1955. I was in the army and driving home from the base, listening to the classical-music station in my yellow Studebaker convertible. The program was interrupted by an announcement that James Dean had been killed on the way to the Laguna Seca raceway. I was stationed at Fort Ord on the Monterey Peninsula less than twenty-five miles from Laguna Seca. Dean had been killed on California Highway 46, later nicknamed Blood Alley because of the number of fatal accidents that happened on that stretch of road. He was driving a Porsche 550 Spyder, which the studio had prohibited him from driving until *Giant,* the film he was shooting, was finished. He was in the car with his mechanic when a station wagon pulled out from a side road. Either he didn't see it, or it was too close for him to avoid the collision. They had to finish some scenes in the film using a double at long range.

Tom Pittman was an up-and-coming young actor in Hollywood when I started my career. He worked often and had developed a fine reputation in the business. He was compared to James Dean and was being groomed to move into that spot. Besides doing movies, he was very active in the Hollywood theater scene, doing plays at the Players' Ring Theatre and other notable venues. One day, he went missing. They searched for him for a couple of weeks and finally found him dead behind the wheel of his Porsche Speedster, hidden in the brush in a canyon adjacent to Laurel Canyon. He had obviously lost control of the car in a curve and had careened down into a deeply wooded part of the canyon, another statistic to add to the number of creative people who died young, such as Elvis Presley, Michael Jackson, James Dean, Heath Ledger, and Marilyn Monroe.

HOLLYWOOD TRAGEDY: IGNORANCE CAN BE FATAL

Jon-Erik Hexum

Jon-Erik Hexum was a young, handsome actor, considered by some in Hollywood to be the "next big thing." He was in demand and turned down roles in "The Dukes of Hazzard," "CHIPs," and many daytime soap operas. He made his debut in the TV series "Voyagers!" and also as the lead opposite Joan Collins in "Making of a Male Model." His final role was Mac Harper in the series "Cover Up." Since he got bored waiting for many hours on the set of that show, he jokingly put a prop .44 Magnum handgun loaded with blanks to his temple and fired. The wadding being propelled with the force of a full-load .44 Magnum blank blew a hole in his temple the size of a quarter. He was rushed to the hospital, where the surgeon worked on him for five hours but described the damage to his brain as life-ending. One week later he was taken off life support and pronounced dead. He had obviously thought that one couldn't get hurt by a blank cartridge!

The prop man should not have let him have the gun before it was needed for the scene. Hexum's ignorance about firearms, about the fact that a blank cartridge can burn you from a distance of four or five feet away, cost him his life. The production company called me to coach his replacement. I was interviewed at the studio, where they told me exactly what had happened. I agreed to work with the replacement and gave them my fee. A couple of days later they called me and told me I would not be needed. I don't know whether they thought that my fee was too high or whether, as I figured out later, they wrote the part of Mac Harper out of the show.

THE JEWISH INDIAN KILLED BY A MEDICINE MAN

Jeff Chandler

His name was Ira Grossel, and he was from Brooklyn. He was strikingly handsome, well over six feet tall, and his hair was prematurely gray. He was an actor, who in his early years did stage work in the East. When he migrated to Hollywood, his name was changed to Jeff Chandler and he began a very successful movie career. In one of his earlier films, *Broken Arrow* with James Stewart, he played the famous Indian chief Cochise. The role afforded him an Oscar nomination. As a matter of fact, he was the first actor ever to be nominated playing an Indian, and he reprised that role in two other films. Hollywood was known for throwing actors into ethnic roles that were quite far from their real ethnic background. Rock Hudson once played an Indian, while Akim Tamiroff, a famous character actor in the forties and fifties with a very thick Russian accent, was cast as a Chinese general, an Italian revolutionary and almost everything but a Russian. If you had an accent in Hollywood, they used you in any role that required an accent other than the one that was yours. Eugenie Leontovich, another Russian, played an Indian princess and a Gypsy of unknown origin in films. In later years real Indians were cast as Indians, as a greater and more authentic concern for reality found its way into Hollywood films.

Jeff Chandler acted in many movies. He played several ethnic characters—an Arab chief in *Flame of Araby,* a Polynesian in *Bird of Paradise*—as well as romantic leads and other types of roles, starring in *Thunder in the Sun* with Susan Hayward, who was a friend from Brooklyn; *War Arrow* with Maureen O'Hara; *Foxfire, Return to Peyton Place*, *Away all Boats,* and *Merrill's Marauders.*

It was on that last film that he injured his back. He had a herniated disk and went into surgery to correct it; but the doctor clipped an artery that receded into a muscle, and he bled to death. The Chandler family sued the doctor and won.

Jeff was just forty-two years old when he died. He was also a singer and had recorded a number of albums and appeared in nightclubs, such as the Riviera in Las Vegas. He had two daughters, both of whom died of cancer. His life was truly tragic. His mother, his uncle, his aunt, and his grandfather also died of cancer. They say that in every life a little rain must fall, but I would say that in Jeff's life it was a tsunami.

ACTOR DIES WHILE SHOOTING FILM

Eric Fleming

Eric Fleming started as a stage actor, first in Chicago then in New York. On Broadway he starred in *My Three Angels, Stalag 17,* and *No Time for Sergeants,* before moving to Hollywood to be on television and in films. Over a period of time he appeared in most of the television series of the period, including "The Web," "Kraft Television Theatre," and "Suspense," and then he landed the lead on "Rawhide," which ran for eight seasons. In 1966 he was cast in a two-part television film called "High Jungle." During the filming he and Nico Minardos were on the Huallaga River in Peru, when their dugout canoe capsized and threw both of them into the water. Minardos managed to swim to shore, but Fleming got caught in the rapids and drowned. His body was not discovered until three days later. The irony of it all, and a tragic comment on life, is that he had bought a ranch in Hawaii and planned to retire when "Rawhide" wrapped. I suppose that his plan included doing that last film.

TOO YOUNG AND TOO TALENTED TO BE MURDERED

Sal Mineo

He was young and talented, but his life was cut short by a low-life drifter who stabbed him to death in an underground parking garage in West Hollywood. The motive was unclear but the result was final.

Sal Mineo was born and raised in New York by Italian immigrant parents. As a young kid he was into street gangs and criminal activities in the tough neighborhoods of the Bronx. Arrested for robbery at age ten, he was given the choice of juvenile confinement or school. He chose the latter and went to an acting school, where his interest in acting began. At sixteen he appeared on Broadway in *The Rose Tattoo* with Eli Wallach and Maureen Stapleton and later in *The King and I* with Yul Brynner. In Hollywood he appeared in a plethora of films, most notably *Rebel without a Cause* with James Dean and Natalie Wood, which was directed by Nicholas Ray and also featured Jim Backus. A side note here: All of the main characters in that film are deceased, including the director. Mineo was also in *Giant* and in *Exodus,* where he played Dov Landau, a role that earned him an Academy Award nomination.

Mineo was just thirty-seven years old when he was killed. It is painful to realize that if he had lived he could have contributed so much more to us. Instead, late at night in a deserted underground garage, he encountered a loser, a drifter named Lionel Ray Williams, who was later caught, convicted of the crime and sentenced to life in prison.

WHO'S ON FIRST

I'm not sure that this qualifies as a Hollywood tragedy, but I think it is definitely tragic. Abbott and Costello were the biggest comedy team in the business throughout the forties, fifties and well into the sixties. Bud Abbott was considered by many people to be one of the greatest straight men in the business. Growing up in those decades, I never missed one of their films. My friend Ronnie and I would take a streetcar or bus and travel to the other side of town to catch those movies. When their careers started on the downslide and they broke up, both of them tried to go it alone, Abbott with a new comic partner and Costello doing serious acting. Abbott died of prostate cancer in 1974, but before he died penniless he took out a small ad in a magazine, which I stumbled on. It said, "If any of you were ever entertained by me and liked our comedy, please send me fifty cents, or if you can afford it, one dollar. I really need the money to survive." When I read that, it brought tears to my eyes, and for years I have not been able to shake the shock that it created for me. I think that it is a Hollywood tragedy!

BLACKLISTING:
WHAT WAS REALLY UN-AMERICAN

THE LEFT AND THE RIGHT IN HOLLYWOOD

The film industry has always been mostly populated by liberals, although there has been a fairly large contingent of conservatives also. For years it was said that the motion-picture industry was run by liberal Jews—the Warner Brothers, Louis B. Mayer, Harry Cohn, Samuel Goldwyn, Irving Thalberg—most of whom were at the helm of a major studio. On the other end of the spectrum there was John Ford with his stable of actors such as John Wayne, Ward Bond, Victor McLaglen and others. In the 1940s Victor McLaglen formed a polo club that was very militaristic and later a motorcycle club with the same overtones. I heard rumors that they wore black shirts and had very conservative values. John Wayne also created a very conservative group aimed at protecting American values. It was called "The Motion Picture Alliance for the Preservation of American Ideals" and was a right-wing political organization. While John Wayne played many military figures in films, to my knowledge he actually never served one minute in any branch of the military. Then there was the John Birch Society, which was extremely conservative—America for Americans. To this day there are organizations that are committed to preserve "the American way" and really believe in what they stand for.

I believe in this country. I love America, and I feel that there is room for the left and the right. It isn't just a two-party system with the Democrats and the Republicans; rather it comes down to how far to the left of the eagle's wings and how far to the right of the eagle's wings people stand. We do, however, have to be aware of the fact that when fascism comes to our country it may be wrapped in the American flag.

In the 1950s a government organization called the House Un-American Activities Committee, headed by Senator McCarthy, was responsible for creating a blacklist that stopped a plethora of actors, writers, and other show-business people from working in their profession. Some of them even committed suicide, while others, such as Robert Taylor and Ronald Reagan, testified in support of the committee. During that dark period when so many actors, directors and writers were blacklisted, writers such as Dalton Trumbo and the rest of the group known as The Hollywood Ten wrote films under assumed names. Movies were made about that period: *The Front, Guilty by Suspicion,* and others. Hollywood has made many other motion pictures that have championed the rights and civil liberties of people, such as *To Kill a Mockingbird,* which addressed racism—black and white—*Gentleman's Agreement,* which explored anti-Semitism in America, and recently *A Time to Kill* and many others. Gregory Peck, a true giant in the defense of liberal and civic values, made a number of films like the ones mentioned above.

KAZAN AND HUAC

During that infamous period of the House Un-American Activities Committee when the government was looking for Communists under every rock, a large number of people in the entertainment business, including stage, film and television people, were questioned. One of them was Kazan. To be considered a "friendly witness" you had to name the names of everyone you knew to have been involved with communist activities. Kazan sang like a bird and put the finger on many people who he knew were involved in some way with subversive activities. His rationalization was that those people had already been named by others who had testified before him. He was quoted as saying that he wanted to work and that that was why he had cooperated. He did work. His career was not ended like that of so many of the people he or others put the finger on. Many lost their careers and income, and some even lost their lives. Philip Loeb, who had been named by someone, was immediately prevented from working. He was on a television sitcom, "The Goldbergs," where he played Molly Goldberg's husband. Molly stopped the production of the show for several weeks in defiance of his being blacklisted. He had been supporting a handicapped child with his work and finally committed suicide.

That's just one story. There were hundreds. When Kazan was on stage at the Academy Awards, accepting some kind of award, many people in the audience sat on their hands and refused to applaud him. As the camera panned the audience, I recognized many famous actors, including Nick Nolte, not applauding or responding positively.

NAMING NAMES

Marc Lawrence, a notable character actor in the forties and fifties, and Jeff Corey, also a successful character actor in Hollywood, both got caught up in the communist thing of the thirties, when so many, who were brainwashed into thinking that they were saving America, either joined the Communist party or became fellow travelers. Marc Lawrence was called up in front of the House Un-American Activities Committee and named Jeff Corey, who in turn refused to name anyone. Both men were blacklisted, however, and kept from working in the business. Jeff became a teacher and gathered a fairly large following of young actors. Marc went to Europe, where he played leads in films, until the blacklist was lifted. He then returned to America and resumed his career.

Since I related my experiences with Jeff Corey earlier, at this juncture I'll only talk about my relationship to Marc Lawrence. I met him at the Actors Studio in Hollywood when I was the head of the directors unit. He observed several sessions that I was moderating and approached me, asking if I would be willing to work with him on a film he was producing and directing. He wanted me to be his assistant, to work with the actors and specifically coach his daughter, who was playing the lead. Originally titled *The Thirteenth Pig* and later I believe retitled *Pigs!* The film was almost totally cast out of the studio. I only worked on it for a couple of weeks but spent a lot of time working with Marc's daughter and was able to get some of my students parts in it.

HE DIED IN THE SADDLE

John Garfield

No, he wasn't a cowboy. I do not believe he ever even did a western. His name was John Garfield, and he was a very talented actor, who was very active and successful in Hollywood in the forties and fifties. He started out as part of the famous Group Theatre and worked on many stage productions. After receiving great acclaim for his performance in *Awake and Sing,* he was lured to Hollywood, where he did scores of films: *Gentleman's Agreement, The Postman Always Rings Twice, Body and Soul, Force of Evil* and *He Ran All the Way,* to name just a few. The lead in *Golden Boy* was written for him but given to William Holden.

Garfield was active in the liberal political social causes which many of the actors working with the Group Theatre were involved in, and he became embroiled in HUAC and the Red Scare of the fifties. The rumor that circulated around Hollywood, and what I had heard for years, was that he had died in a New York hotel room having sex with a woman the night before he was scheduled to testify in front of HUAC. After doing some research and reading his biographies, however, I found a somewhat different story. He actually did testify in front of the committee in April 1951. He told them that he had never been a member of the Communist party and that he was not a Communist. He refused to name names, and because of that he was blacklisted. The day before Garfield's death Clifford Odets testified before HUAC and totally reaffirmed that Garfield had never been in the Communist party.

Born of Jewish parents, with the name Jacob Julius Garfinkle, John died at the age of thirty-nine. He did actually die in the saddle, having sex with a former showgirl in her home. Her name was Iris Whitney.

John experienced a number a tragedies in his life besides being blacklisted: His six-year-old daughter Katherine died and, according to my research, he never recovered from her death. He had two other children: a son, David, and another daughter, Julie. I worked with David in a pilot for a television show many years ago. He was the spitting image of his father and about a foot taller. I also met Julie in New York a few years ago at a theater seminar. We had never met before but knew of each other's reputation as teachers. She was beautiful and charming. When I asked her about David, she told me that he had died several years earlier as a result of drugs. I was very sad to hear that news.

Even though John had a history of heart problems, what he had to go through and tolerate I am sure hastened his demise. I love this country, but I am ashamed of that period and all the lives that were ruined during that witch hunt.

SENATOR MCCARTHY'S GHOST IS STILL HAUNTING HOLLYWOOD

A different sort of blacklist exists also in Hollywood, but it is undercover and operates as a secret in the shadows. For example, Aaron Spelling kept a little book in which he would make notations about actors and others who had somehow offended him. He would then put out the word to other powerful producers not to hire those people. He, of course, was not the only one. Harry Cohn, the head of Columbia Studios, was famous for blacklisting actors, as was Warner Brothers. In fact, a book has been written about Cohn called *King Cohn.* Alfred Hitchcock ruined the career of an actress who refused to sleep with him; television shows have been cancelled because some powerful executive got his nose bent out of shape. Except for big stars, actors are at the bottom of the totem pole and most vulnerable to blacklisting.

A while ago one of my students told me an unnerving story, one that was hard to believe but real. A close friend of his, also an actor who worked fairly regularly, got involved with an actress in a class they were both in. They were working on a love scene and over the course of several weeks of rehearsal ended up carrying that scene into their real lives. At first, he refused to get involved, knowing that her husband was a very big producer in the film industry, who not only wielded a great deal of power but had personal friends who, for the most part, were also hugely influential. However, when their blood ran too hot, they ended up in a small room in an out-of-the-way motel. It was a one-time thing, which, as he related the experience to my student, fell far below expectations. She was older than he and had done this numerous times with other men, mostly actors she worked with.

One evening, when she and her husband were into a very heavy argument, he pushed her into naming the names of all her infidelities, and, as a result, this young actor friend of my student's was blacklisted. He stopped getting auditions and stopped working. Essentially his acting career was over. He hung around Hollywood for a couple of years trying to get work, but without success. He finally gave up the business, moved to New York, did some plays and a few commercials, and ended up choosing to go into another field.

That is not as uncommon as one would think. It goes on every day. An actor might refuse a role and offend the producer or the director, or he might insult someone in a powerful place. I know an actor, a really talented actor, who insulted his way right out of the business. The word went out on him and he couldn't *buy* a job.

AARON SPELLING'S LITTLE BLACK BOOK

A number of years ago Spelling was involved with an actress, Carolyn Jones. I'm not sure, but they may have been married. She was in the hospital for something, and he kept a little book listing all of the people who didn't show up to visit her. What he did with those names I really don't know. I just heard the story and imagined the rest. Power corrupts, and it is rampant in Hollywood.

SEX IN HOLLYWOOD
OR SOME LIKE IT HOT

SEX IN HOLLYWOOD; SEX TRADING

Entire books could be written on many of the short Hollywood stories in this book. I have been teaching acting for fifty-two years, and a lot of people have been through my classes. In private lessons some of them have really opened up to me and, knowing that their privacy was assured, related some of the most shocking stories.

It is a commonly known fact that the people in positions of power who have the ability to hire actors have used those positions to acquire sex from desperate young actors wanting to work. It is a "carrot" held out, and quite often girls, and sometimes guys, will get on their backs and fuck for the job.

One of my students came up with an interesting way to avoid getting sexually involved with men attempting to seduce her for a promise of work: After being approached, she would say, "If I do that for work, what would I do for fun?" It almost always cooled the situation down. She was committed not to succumb to the advances.

GO AWAY, HAVE A "FUCK FEST" AND CLIMB YOUR WAY TO STARDOM

A beautiful and talented young woman in my class, eager to make it in Hollywood and who would do anything it took to do it, went to Big Sur for the weekend with a producer who had promised her a very good part in a film he was about to do. Lo and behold, she got the part, which started a pretty successful career! Sex is a commodity.

COME TAKE AN OCEAN CRUISE WITH ME

Hearsay is not allowed in the courtroom, but it has never been absent from Hollywood. Here is a story told to me by a friend: Janice Rule, whom I knew, told my friend about a successful Hollywood producer who used the name S.P. Eagle to lure beautiful young actresses onto his boat, promising to give them work. He would then seduce them to have a kind of very kinky sex with him: Instead of conventional fucking, he would have them undress and defecate on his chest. A very well-trained and experienced psychologist might be able to explain that phenomenon.

Janice was married to Ben Gazzara for some years and had a fairly successful career of her own.

SEX WITH A WAR HERO

This experience took place in either the late sixties or the early seventies. This very attractive woman—late twenties, with beautiful raven hair and big brown eyes, slim with a very nice figure and a wonderful smile exposing a perfect set of gleaming white teeth—who looked as if she came from a wholesome home with doting parents and possibly taught kindergarten or first grade, expressed a desire to study acting but never made it clear that she wanted to pursue it as a career. I often wondered why she was taking private lessons with me but later figured that she was desperately lonely and needed someone to talk to who would really listen to her. It was just a short time before I realized that she wasn't anything like the way she looked. She was not wholesome but really troubled, with very strange habits, friends and needs. I suggested that she seek counseling with a qualified therapist and repeatedly told her that I was an acting teacher and not a psychiatrist. She told me that she had been to several therapists and had found them to be negative and judgmental, and that anyway she needed someone like me who seemed to understand and not judge her. Our working relationship didn't last that long, because I was very uncomfortable being put in the position of a therapist. We had three sessions, and I convinced her to move on, which she did reluctantly. In those three sessions she told me that she needed to be burned with a cigarette in order to achieve an orgasm, and upon telling me that, she rolled up her sleeves and exposed the burn scars in various states of healing. There were at least twenty on both arms. I tried to conceal my shock and instead became comforting and understanding. It was one of my better acting jobs!

Neville Brand

She went on to tell me that she had a relationship with a fairly well-known actor and that she would visit him a couple of times each week. I don't remember whether she mentioned having intercourse with him, but she did tell me that she gave him "brown showers" on a regular basis. After hearing her story, I asked if she would tell me who the actor was, and after very little coaxing she told me that it was Neville Brand. I was shocked. I knew who he was and had seen him in many movies. He was one of the most decorated soldiers in World War II. The story, or what might have been Hollywood folklore, was that at night he would sneak behind enemy lines and kill those soldiers with a knife, returning to base in the early hours of the morning covered with blood. What makes me think that his exploits might have actually happened was that many years later a director I knew, Denis Sanders, did a film called *War Hunt* starring John Saxon, who played a soldier who did sneak behind enemy lines to kill the enemy and return at sunrise. I recently spoke to someone who knew Neville Brand well, and he said that after the war and as the years passed, Brand became an alcoholic and lived in a seedy motel off Hollywood Boulevard. I wonder if his tragic life was the result of the trauma caused by the war.

BS AROUND THE FIREPLACE

This story was told to me by Erik Holland, whom I introduced earlier in this book:

"After a few days on 'Remington Steele' we had an evening shoot at CBS in the Valley. Somehow there was a primitive location between a dozen or so large stages. So on a little hill with a creek running nearby, the crew had set up a nice fireplace for the extras, mostly a scruffy bunch who acted as background for me, the boss, a German winegrower around Riverside somewhere.

"In the group of extras was an older fellow named Don, who was telling a story about John Garfield and Lana Turner in *The Postman Always Rings Twice.* For those who have seen the movie, Don was the blond young man who brings Lana in on a wheelchair for a courtroom scene around the end of the movie. He didn't have any lines, but he looked good, Lana thought, so soon he was visiting her in her trailer day in and day out. She was drop-dead beautiful and a sexual wild woman. Don fell madly in love with her. The affair lasted a few weeks, and then she had to go on location in Laguna Beach for some beach shots. He missed her terribly, and when she came back, he ran to her trailer and knocked on the door. It seems she was entertaining someone else inside, so she told Don to 'beat it' and not come around anymore. He was heartbroken for months afterwards and didn't see her again for thirty or so years.

"Cut to a nice little restaurant/bar in Paradise Cove. He is at the bar with his grown son. The bartender says, 'There is a lady and her grown daughter at a table, and they'd like you to join them.'

"Don recognizes Lana and her daughter (who has had some very adverse publicity), and he replies, 'Only if you send over some drinks for them.' He sits next to Lana. The years have not been good to her. She reaches over, places her hand on his arm, looks into his eyes, pauses and says, 'Whatever happened to Don?'

"During the war years Don was under contract to MGM. He was 4F and therefore not draftable, but because he was so handsome, MGM thought they could make him an actor. It never happened. Around the same time, there were rumors that Van Johnson was gay, not a good thing to be at the time. Well, Don was Van's stand-in and had the key to his dressing room, which Don used from time to time with one of the hotties who were always around. One evening he was in Van's room going down on a cutie with his back to the door, when the cleaning lady opened the door, gasped and shut the door. MGM was like a family house, and when the word got to Louis B. Mayer that Van had been caught red-handed, Don's contract was extended another year!"

TWO BEAUTIFUL WOMEN MAKING LOVE TO EACH OTHER

This is a rumor that circulated throughout Hollywood for many years. It was by accident that Frank Sinatra discovered Ava Gardner and Lana Turner in bed together doing the "double-backed beast." Frank was madly in love with Ava, and one can't help but wonder what his reaction was.

There are scores of stories about the homosexual and bisexual activities of the Hollywood stars. Some of the names that have come to the surface would shock movie goers. Sigmund Freud would have had a field day attempting to analyze the motivation behind the bizarre sexual activities of those iconic figures. For decades the sexual orientation and behavior of many of the top box-office stars were protected by the studio PR departments, and press agents were hired to keep the actors' names out of the newspapers.

In 1941 Jane Russell did a film called *The Outlaw.* In one scene she gets into bed with a dying man to keep him warm. She was fully clothed, but it still caused a furor! It was racy and crossed the line of what was acceptable behavior in films. Because it was difficult to pass the Hollywood censor boards, the movie was released two years after the 1941 filming and only achieved popularity in 1946. It was a box-office smash.

The Victorian attitude of our society in the forties and fifties imposed stringent limitations on what could be seen on the screen. A kiss between two characters could only last for seven seconds; two married characters in a film had to sleep in twin beds. They were not allowed to share the same bed. Nudity in any form—even the suggestion of an exposed breast—was censored and did not show up in the movie theaters. Alfred Hitchcock had difficulty releasing the sex scene in *Psycho,* even though both characters had underwear on. She is wearing a bra and a full slip and he is in boxer shorts.

We have come a very long way in what we can now show on the screen. Several television shows and series are openly exploring and exposing the activities of homosexuals, including a new cable show exclusively focused on men looking for romantic relationships with other men. Sex sells, and anything in the film industry that makes money is fair game. Name actors are now totally nude in scenes, often in bed making love with someone who is also nude.

HE HAD THE NAVY JOIN HIM

Liberace was a very gifted pianist, who achieved great success in concerts, in movies and on television. He was very flamboyant, always wore wild costumes, and played his unique signature piano, on top of which sat a lavish candelabrum. He did soundtrack work for movies and even appeared in a few of them. His biography in IMDb states that for most of his life he was a closeted homosexual. Well, I am sure that the closet must have had see-through glass walls, because he was so obviously gay in his mannerisms and speech that a blind deaf-mute would have known of his sexual preferences! It is difficult for someone who is famous to hide his sexual orientation, and I believe he didn't do a very good job of it.

In the sixties, seventies, and even into the eighties homosexuality was the kiss of death to a performer, an actor, and anyone else in the public eye. Many homosexual movie stars were seen publicly with women hanging on their arm and were even encouraged by their studio to get married just to avoid rumors. Rock Hudson was one of the actors who were notorious homosexuals, and his studio and its publicity department were constantly fielding rumors, hearsay and gossip to avoid exposure, which would have totally destroyed his career. In the nineties and now in the twenty-first century homosexuality is obviously more acceptable.

The rumors about Liberace circulated around Hollywood for years, and he was paired with numerous famous personalities, but his appetite to procure new conquests drove him to very imaginative approaches. He was very successful and had a great deal of money, so he hired people to go to the shipyards and invite sailors back to his home, enticing them with lavish banquets of food and alcohol. The sailors would arrive, imbibe and watch pornography on a big screen in one of Liberace's enormous rooms; and while at first the pornography was heterosexual, it eventually turned homosexual. At that point many of the sailors headed for the door, but the few that lingered were Liberace's targets. If they stayed to watch the homosexual activity, they were probably interested and could be approached and most likely seduced.

At present I am reading a book called *Sex at Dawn.* While the title may be a little bit misleading, I believe that it means sex at the dawning of mankind and from prehistoric man millions of years ago to the present. While Sigmund Freud has been maligned and discredited by many psychologists for his seeming preoccupation with sex, the book traces the profound sexual force that has driven man, and it probably validates some of Freud's sexual theories. This study of sex through millions of years has been given the name of "evolutionary psychology," and while many of the so-called discoveries are just theories, there is real evidence that some of them draw a real picture of the sexual appetites of man for the millions of years they are exploring.

THE GAY BILLIONAIRE

He was affable, gregarious and liked by almost everyone. A little fat boy who grew up in San Mateo near San Francisco, he displayed musical talent from the very beginning, and to be a musical movie star was what he always wanted. He carried his father's name, Mervin Griffin. For many years he remained a fat boy, until people he was impressed with told him that he would never be successful in show business until he slimmed down, so he did. He started out professionally as a singer for Freddy Martin's band. It was the era of the big bands, each of which had a lead singer, many of whom went on to become famous personalities in their own right. Often, the band played at the famous Coconut Grove, where the elite of Hollywood would wine and dine. Many of the singers Merv admired frequented the club. He would be invited to join them after a set, and he thus made many friends in the business.

Merv Griffin

Merv's real passion was to be as successful as Gordon MacRae, who was a huge musical film star. That fame eluded Merv, however, and that was a source of great disappointment for him. He spent a good part of his younger life being broke. He took singing jobs and at one point was the host of a Catholic talk show, which he wasn't too keen on doing. He did do a film with Kathryn Grayson, a very big singing star in the movies of the fifties, but unfortunately, his entire time on screen was very short, and the film did absolutely nothing to promote his career.

As I mentioned before, Merv was a really nice guy and most people took to him. He rarely had any conflicts, but he did break a couple of hearts and had his broken quite frequently. According to a biography I read about him, he was a promiscuous homosexual, but he was in the closet most of his life and was quite often seen with a woman on his arm, especially Eva Gabor, who was one of his closest friends. He projected the image of a heterosexual man, but his secret life was outrageous. He had brief or ongoing homosexual affairs with almost everyone in Hollywood—big stars such as Peter Lawford, Robert Walker, Marlon Brando, Wally Cox, Tom Drake—whose heart he broke when he dumped him—and Rock Hudson, to name a few. As I mentioned above, Rock was also kept buried in the closet, so that his homosexuality would not affect his career, but he was an outrageous sexual prowler with an insatiable sexual appetite. Errol Flynn was another one of Merv's partners, even though Flynn was also heterosexual and had many exploits with women, even underage ones. Roddy McDowall and Merv also became great friends, and McDowall was a wonderful source for Merv's sexual needs. It was even rumored that Howard Hughes was one of Merv's lovers.

A lot of straight actors gladly drop their pants to get a part in a film, and the homosexual predators take advantage of their position to conquer and seduce their prey. One of those despicable characters was Henry Willson, a Hollywood talent agent, who created a stable of actors whose names he would change. Rock Hudson was one of his clients. Rock's real name was Roy Fitzgerald—and what was wrong with that name? I saw Willson at the Factory a couple of times. He was falling down drunk and flirting with all the young boys who were there.

At one point, Merv was hired to replace a singer on the Robert Q. Lewis show on TV. Lewis didn't really like Merv and thought that he had a mediocre singing voice, but it was on that show that Merv met, and in 1958 married, Lewis's secretary, Julann Elisabeth Wright. They had a son, Tony, but were divorced in 1976. For Merv, who had fought to hide his homosexuality for most of his life and had purposely been seen with women on his arm in public, marriage and subsequent fatherhood were probably an attempt to further his image as a heterosexual man, even though all of his lovers—and there were scores of them—knew the truth. The rumors circulated around New York and Hollywood, but the insiders seem to have kept the truth under their hats in respect for him.

Merv was finally offered second position on "The Morning Show," an early morning talk show. When the host of that show was let go by CBS, Merv moved into the first position and proved that he was a great interviewer and entertainer. Sometime later he hosted his own show, "The Merv Griffin Show," which enjoyed tremendous popularity for many years.

Merv's real financial success, however, came with his creation of various game shows, such as "Jeopardy" and "Wheel of Fortune." Both shows ran for a long time and were even revived after they had gone off the air. They are still running today. What had eluded Merv throughout his life was finally there for him, a lot of money, which he intelligently invested in property and other lucrative ventures. Like his hero, Howard Hughes, he too became a billionaire. I really believe that he would have been happier with a lot less money, however, if only he could have accomplished his lifelong dream of being a musical movie star like Gordon MacRae.

PORNOGRAPHY IN HOLLYWOOD

Many actors who come to Hollywood with big dreams of stardom spend a number of years trying to crack through the wall, going from one audition to another, if indeed they are lucky enough to find an agent willing to take on newcomers and get them out there. After several years of mounting disappointments and becoming exhausted from working in restaurants to survive, some of them are lured into acting in pornographic films. When I was a teenager growing up in Chicago, those movies were called *stag films,* and when we were lucky enough to get hold of one, a group of horny boys would come over to my house, and we would set up an eight-millimeter projector in my rumpus room in the basement and watch the movie. It was a time in our society when getting girls to give it up was next to impossible. They were all saving their virginity for the wedding bed. So we had to satisfy our raging hormones with stag films and masturbation.

Times have surely changed. There are porno theaters in almost every city in the country now, and the Internet is flooded with pornographic sites. Unfortunately, most actors who get involved in those films never make the transition to regular movies. There have been some exceptions, but I only know of a couple of them: Joan Crawford, who was known to have done some exotic films in her very early years, came a long way from those skin flicks to the star she became, ultimately ending up as Mrs. Pepsi Cola. Traci Lords, another actor who started in porno films and was very successful in that genre, even making a name for herself as a porno actor, moved into movies such as *Cry Baby* with Johnny Depp and also did quite well on television. I caught a couple of her performances on the tube, and I have to say she was pretty good.

On the other hand, Linda Lovelace, who did *Deep Throat,* a film that grossed millions of dollars, was only paid twelve hundred dollars for her work in that film. That was all she ever saw from the gigantic financial returns. She died broke and never realized any of her dreams. Marilyn Chambers, another porn actor, who had filmed the very popular *Behind the Green Door,* also died without ever fulfilling her acting dreams.

A number of years ago I received a call from John Holmes, a famous porn star. He wanted to come and train with me but never showed up. He died shortly after that call. There are endless stories about people who are drawn into the glamour of Hollywood only to wake up to the reality of how competitive and difficult it is to succeed in this business.

The porn industry has become more dignified by presenting itself as the “adult film industry,” and it is indeed an industry. Some estimates say that it brings in ten billion dollars a year worldwide and contributes hundreds of millions of dollars to the Los Angeles economy. It has come a very long way from the hard-to-get underground stag films that I watched as a teenager to the glitzy fuck films it produces now.

Each year the industry has its own awards show, patterned after the Oscars and the Golden Globes. This year their twelfth annual awards affair took place at the Hyatt Regency Century Plaza Hotel. Riley Reid, a twenty-two-year-old porn actor won for the best female performer of the year and was quoted as saying that she was proud of being so good at what she does. Dozens of performers posed for photographers and signed autographs, and thirty-five awards were presented: best girl-girl award, male sex toy of the year, and so on. As they do on other award shows, the nominees came in gowns designed by known designers.

A FUNNY THING HAPPENED ON THE WAY TO THE STUDIO

WHAT PRICE COMEDY?

We often wonder what makes comedians and comic actors funny and what their lives must be like: Are they constantly making people laugh? Are their spouses and children forever entertained by their wit and humor? I am not sure what I thought until I was able to experience several comic actors firsthand. In 1963 I auditioned and got a running role on "The New Phil Silvers Show," which was the second series Phil did. The first one, which was done in New York in 1955 and in which Phil played Sergeant Bilko, was one of the most successful television series ever. Many of his lines in that show became standard one-liners.

I had gotten the audition as a result of teaching Phil's wife, Evelyn Silvers, formally known as Evelyn Patrick, a beautiful woman who was the spokesperson for Revlon cosmetics. She had come to my class to study acting and was quite serious about it. We became friends, and my wife and I were very often invited to the Silvers' home in Beverly Hills. I really liked Phil. He was quite a nice guy and very accepting of me and my family. I had a boy and a girl, while the Silvers had five girls. We spent many Sundays in their backyard watching the children play together.

As a result of our relationship I was invited to audition for the new show they were casting. I knew that I had to deliver and that our friendship would have no bearing on my getting the job if I was not able to do it. The audition took place in a small room at 20th Century Fox. Four or five of us were asked to follow a situation and improvise with Phil. I jumped in and was all over the place. At one point I climbed on top of a table and began shouting and behaving animatedly to fit the description of the character we had been given. Rod Amateau, the director, started laughing so hard he interrupted the audition. When I left, I had mixed feelings about whether I had done well. Had I been too audacious? Had I made a fool of myself? Would this get in the way of our friendship? Did Phil think I was too pushy? I'm sure that every actor reading this will identify with all that I felt after the audition. When I pulled into the driveway of my house in the Valley, my wife was standing there, arms wildly flailing in the air, shouting, "You got it!" And so started my education about working in a series and meeting Phil and Evelyn's friends.

I had been working as an actor sporadically before that, not earning enough to depend solely on acting. In those days SAG minimum was a little over a hundred dollars a day. I really don't remember what I was paid for my part in the show, but it wasn't very much. That is not to say that I wasn't totally elated to have landed the job. I was! I felt that it might be the beginning of a successful acting career.

I was thrust into a society alien to my understanding and way out of my league. The list of people might have read like a *Who's Who in Hollywood.* It included famous actors, producers and agents, all of whom lived in Beverly Hills, one house being larger and more impressive than another. Polly Bergen was married to Freddie Fields, a well-known, very successful agent and producer. Barbara Rush was part of that group. I later worked in a television show with her and found her to be a really good person. The women had dresses and gowns designed for them by famous designers at a cost of twenty-five hundred dollars apiece, and the fact that they could wear each dress or gown only once was hard for me to fathom, since at that time my yearly income was about five thousand dollars.

Since Phil wore very thick glasses and did not see well, on several occasions he asked me to drive him to the studio. He would really open up to me about his life and express many of his dissatisfactions and problems. I sat silently listening, not contributing anything. He seemed quite sad on those trips from home to the studio. I wondered how he was able to switch gears and be so funny on camera. Then I remembered what Lucy had shared with us: "That's acting!" I loved Phil and felt a lot for him and the things he shared with me. It was my first real experience with comedians and comic actors. I guess up to that point I had been naïve about what made them funny, thinking that it was the way they were.

On several occasions I was invited to Phil's house, which was filled with famous comics and comedy personalities. One evening the group consisted of Phil, Groucho Marx, Buddy Hackett, and Herbie Faye, a close friend of Phil's from the old days, who had been on the original show in 1955. Other comedians were also there. Groucho was old and didn't seem well. He was with his much younger wife and he said very little, but it was easy to see that he was not a happy man. Buddy Hackett was "on," throwing one-liners and competitively telling jokes. He too seemed driven and insecure. Phil didn't say much but understood his friends. I sat silently in a corner of the room, feeling way out of my comfort zone. Herbie Faye was not actually a comic actor but had been thrust into comedy roles. That evening I think he felt obligated to contribute and tell a humorous story. I liked Herbie, who was sixty-two years old at the time. He had assumed the role of protector of Phil. At any time, on set or off, if Phil seemed to be in any discomfort, Herbie would jump in and act as a shield. He was a hypochondriac and was always expecting to have a heart attack. He would frequently check his pulse and on several occasions became pale and would sit down. It was fear, not a heart attack. The funny thing is that he lived for thirty more years and died at ninety-two!

On a few occasions Jonathan Winters appeared at Phil's house, and while I didn't feel that he was depressed or unhappy, I thought that he was a little strange. While he was talking to one of Phil's daughters, I think I overheard him tell her that God was a book or something that strange. I cannot remember all of the things he said, but they were beyond weird!

Once, Evelyn invited our class to the Silvers' home for a party. Phil and some of their friends were there and it was a fun evening.

Jack Benny was present, and I must say that of all the comedians I had met through Phil, he appeared to be the most stable and well adjusted. He seemed totally comfortable and was interested in me and my students. He asked a lot of questions about the class and what I taught and was very curious about everyone.

Phil belonged to a membership club in Beverly Hills that was populated by the richest, most famous, and most successful people in and out of the industry. He and most of the others would spend several evenings there playing poker. It was discovered later that the club had their people upstairs above the poker tables spying with scopes on the players' cards. They bilked the players out of tens of thousands of dollars, and I'm sure that Phil lost a bundle.

The series wasn't successful. It had tried to imitate the original show, in which Phil, as Sergeant Bilko, manipulated his way around the army, breaking all the rules and having a ball doing it. The format didn't work in civilian life, so the show was taken out of the factory setting and moved to Phil's house, with a totally different format. That didn't work either. My participation in that short-lived series was over after I had appeared in only a few segments. I think it was one of the biggest disappointments I had experienced up to that time. Of course, it was followed by many more over the years.

I also worked in a film with Dick Shawn. We had a scene together, and he seemed like a happy guy, at least while we were working, but I had heard that he wasn't so. John Belushi, another funny man, died of a drug overdose, as did Chris Farley. There were rumors that Jack Carson was very depressed and drank to excess. Lennie Bruce was found dead of an overdose. Many of the newer comics got involved with drugs and also died of an overdose. So was it comedy or tragedy that all of those comedians experienced?

EMBARRASSING MOMENTS

WHAT'S THE NAME OF THAT ARTIST?

An embarrassing moment occurred several years ago when I was invited up to Jack Nicholson's house in the hills of Beverly Hills. At that time Jack owned two houses on the property. As the story goes, he had bought the second house because its owner would come up the driveway at all hours of the night, bombarding Jack's house with his bright headlights and often waking him up from a sound sleep. After Marlon Brando, who had a house close to Jack's, died, Jack bought that house too. So he now has three houses on the compound.

Jack and I go way back. We were in Martin Landau's acting class together for a couple of years from 1959 to 1960, and after I started teaching he came to my class for a while. We have remained friends for half a century. Driving up Mulholland in my Porsche leaning into the sharp curves was less exciting than my anticipated visit with Jack. I had never been to his house before, so the thought of spending time with him in his domain was especially intriguing. When I arrived at the large, imposing gate, which seemed to be ten feet high, I pressed the button on the arm that reached out, and magically the gate opened. I drove up the driveway, and there was Jack, standing in front of the entrance to his house with his arms outstretched to greet me. We hugged and I was ushered into the house, which was very beautiful—not terribly large but nicely appointed with fine art everywhere. Jack showed me around. In the living room a Picasso painting was adorning the wall. We stopped and looked at it for some time. I immediately recognized the signature, and without a moment of thought passing through the convulsions of my brain, I asked Jack if it was a real Picasso! Gently tipping his head back, he looked at me from the bottom of his eyelids, in vintage Nicholson, and with that look that only Jack can produce said, "Yeah…Eric…it's real." At that very moment I felt the blood rushing into my head much like the water bursting through a hole in a dam. I smiled and hoped that we could have an instant replay of that moment to delete my comment! I really don't know where it had come from, since I knew that Jack had many millions of dollars in his art collection. Even now, years later, I am affected by my response and sincerely hope that he does not remember that moment.

SO, I'M A METHOD ACTOR WORKING TO GET A SENSE OF A LEOPARD

In 1969 I auditioned and got a leading role in a two-part "Kraft Suspense Theater," where I played an assassin whose name was Tippo, an important clue to what he was like. At one point Jan Merlin, whose character was called Jon, says to me, "You know, Tippo, whenever you enter or leave a room, no one knows that you have been there!" That was an important clue for me as an actor to create stealth in my movement as my name indicated—Tippo, tiptoe. So I decided to use an animal as the spine of my character. For several days I went to the zoo to study a black leopard, to watch its rhythms, centers and tempo and create a sense of that animal through my own body. Once I had achieved that, I could translate all of it into human behavior, retaining the sense of the leopard in human form. While on the set, I had to reinvest in getting a sense of the animal by getting down on all fours and walking like a leopard to insure that I could retain the sense of it and translate it into my character's movements and behavior. I did that frequently, whenever I found a private space so I could do it unobserved.

Before a fairly important scene I was to be in, I located a set, a room that wasn't being used, and I bent down and began to work for the animal. I was so involved with my process that I was unaware that the crew had come by and removed a wall of that set, exposing me to the entire cast and crew. There I was, crawling around on the floor like the animal, when I realized that forty people were transfixed looking at me. It was one of those moments when time seems to stop and becomes a freeze frame. I stood up in slow motion, with my back to all of the people watching me, and I slowly walked away. I don't know what they thought, since no one ever mentioned the episode.

ARE YOU A WRITER?

As you may recall, I used to go to New York every other weekend to do weekend workshops and, as artistic director of the American New Theater, to oversee the rehearsals or performances of plays done by its New York branch. The flights to and from New York were often long and tedious; so after reading everything

I could get my hands on, I would involve myself by looking out the window, attempting to identify anything that seemed familiar.

On one of those arduous flights I was sitting next to a middle-aged man scrupulously involved in making notes on a yellow legal pad. I watched his actions for a while and broke the silence by asking him if he was a writer, to which he replied in an almost inaudible voice, "Yes, I am a writer." At that point I felt obligated to tell him that my brother Ed was also a screenwriter and had written many films. Maybe I was just making conversation and maybe I was trying to impress that guy. Some minutes went by, and finally I asked him his name. In the same soft, almost inaudible voice he responded, "Neil Simon."

At that point I was completely and totally embarrassed, unable to speak. I finally managed to utter, "Oh yes, I have heard of you," and quickly turned my head into the window.

You have all seen those cartoons where the animal flattens out and slithers down a flight of stairs; that is exactly how I felt in that moment: I wanted to slither down under the seat. When I said I had heard of him, I could not think fast enough to add, Oh, my God, I love your plays and I have my students do monologues from many of them. Instead, I sat silent for the rest of the flight and never made eye contact with him again.

This story has an interesting addendum though: On the same flight, without my knowing it, was Michael Connors with whom I went way back. Michael had two very successful television series, "Tightrope" and "Mannix," and had also done some films. As I mentioned before, we had met in 1957 or '58 when we were in *Girls of Summer* at the Players' Ring. At the time, he was going by the name of Touch Connors because of his athletic fame in college. A number of years after I had started teaching, he came to me to work on an audition for a film. We were with the same agent at the time.

I ran into him as I was deplaning. We were both headed for the city, so we shared a taxi into town. On the way, I related the story about Neil Simon, whom he knew. Evidently they were good enough friends for Michael to refer to him as "Doc," which I guess was a nickname Simon's friends knew him by. After listening to my story, Michael had a good-natured laugh and related some of his own embarrassing experiences.

NEIL SIMON, NEIL SIMON

Many years after that embarrassing experience with Neil Simon I was having dinner with my wife at a Beverly Hills Italian restaurant that we frequent. I was well into my *pasta marinara* when I lifted my head from the plate and saw Neil Simon enter the restaurant with a somewhat attractive woman. My eyes followed them to a table three or four behind our own. Impulsively I wiped the marinara off my face, got up, walked to their table and said, "Mr. Simon, I just wanted to come by and tell you that I so admire your work. You are a preeminent American playwright and I have enjoyed all of your work. I am so honored to be able to tell you how talented you are and what a fantastic contribution you have made to the American theater. I apologize for interrupting your dinner!"—at which point he said, "No, go ahead, interrupt my dinner some more." I managed a big smile and departed.

WHAT'S THAT IN YOUR MOUTH? A COUGH DROP? GET RID OF IT!

It was 1959, and I was taking a class from Martin Landau, who had come out from New York to Los Angeles with a play, *Middle of the Night,* and had then decided to stay and begun to teach an acting class. I had met Marty at the Players' Ring Theatre, where I had a small part in a play his wife Barbara was in. Marty would show up every night, and we would talk during the intermission. I had told him that I was very frustrated about my training and was thinking of going to New York to study with Lee Strasberg. I really could not financially afford to do that, however, and I shared my frustration with him. He told me that he was teaching a class and invited me to come and audit it. I watched his class, which took place on a Monday evening in a little studio theater on Gardner, off Melrose. My first impression was that they were all nuts! They were doing strange exercises, weird emotional expurgations, and scenes with terminology that was foreign to me. Unfortunately, I was in a kind of catch-22: I was in the play at the Players' Ring probably for another month or two, so if I didn't take the class I would feel uncomfortable with Marty and with Barbara, with whom

I had all of my scenes. So I enrolled in Marty's class. The second time I attended I began to see things that piqued my interest, and by the third session I was hooked. After being there for a while, I was able to find the *how* I had been looking for and not finding in other training venues.

The week after I joined the class Jack Nicholson came into it. I had seen Jack around town and had crossed paths with him at auditions, but at the time I only knew him in passing and to wave to. A lot of other talented people were attending Marty's class: Harry Dean Stanton, Frank Wolff, Shirley Knight, Dick Bradford. A bunch of us really bonded and formed an out-of-class relationship. Every Monday night after class we would go over to Jack's house on Fountain Avenue, and Harry Dean Stanton would play the guitar and sing. We would talk about acting until the sun came up. Jack was involved with a beautiful little girl named Georgiana, who would hang out with us until her eyes got heavy, and would then disappear into the bedroom.

There was a guy in the class—and I am sure every acting class has someone like that—who always looked as if he were confused by life. His hair always looked as though he had just gotten out of bed, and he sometimes appeared to be staring at some faraway place. His name was Ed. In the studio was a little heater that stood against the wall, near the entrance but completely out of the way. Every evening at the beginning of the session, Ed came through the door and stumbled over that heater, making a God-awful racket. It became a weekly event. When we heard his encounter with the heater, everyone knew that Ed had entered the room. One evening, while he was about to do an exercise on the stage and looked as if he was eating or sucking on something, Marty asked him what he had in his mouth, to which Ed responded, "A cough drop." Marty told him to get rid of it, at which point Ed extended his left hand, palm up and ready to receive the half-dissolved cough drop, which he then proceeded to spit out to the right instead! The cough drop went flying out of his mouth and landed on the stage. To say the least, everyone, especially Jack, fell on the floor laughing. To this day, whenever I see Jack, he puts his left hand, palm up, out to the side and fakes spitting something out to the right, which always cracks me up. Many many years later, I heard that

Ed was teaching acting in New York, and oh, my God, would I have liked to be a fly on the wall of that class!

IN THE TOILET WITH TENNESSEE WILIAMS

I recounted before how, in 1954, Lee Blattner, a Northwestern University buddy, and I had driven out from Chicago to become Hollywood movie stars. As naïve as that sounds, we really believed that even if we did not achieve stardom immediately, we would at least get acting work in the first weeks after landing in Hollywood. We had met Joe Mell, who had been in Los Angeles for a number of years, was working in small parts in films and television, and also worked for Meyer Mishkin, an established Hollywood actors' agent. Joe had gotten us jobs at the Players' Ring as stage managers for *The Rose Tattoo* by Tennessee Williams. Because of the great technical preparation Lee and I had from Northwestern and our summer-stock experience, we had easily taken over as stage managers.

The play had an interesting cast: Penny Santon played the leading female role, while Jerry Riggio was the male leading character. The other roles were done by Susan Kohner—the daughter of a famous talent agent, Paul Kohner, and of a beautiful foreign actress—and Jody McCrea, who played her boyfriend. Jody was the son of Joel McCrea and Francis Dee. A tall, very good-looking guy, he was the nicest man I had ever met. One might think that the child of two very famous actors of the period would have been quite arrogant, but there was not a hint of that. Susan later went on to become a very popular working actor. She starred in the film *To Hell and Back* with Audie Murphy and a host of other movies.

Lee and I divided the duties of stage management. He spent most of the time in the light booth, making sure that all the cues were addressed, while I worked to get the actors ready to go on stage and made sure that all the props were in place ready to use in each scene.

The Players' Ring Theatre was configured in a square. The stage was in the middle, and the audience sat on all four sides of it and was so close to the actors in each scene that sometimes, when one of the players was reaching for an object, a member of the audience would pick it up and hand it to him! We played to full houses almost every night and even in the matinees.

One evening at intermission I went to the men's room to relieve myself. There were two stalls next to each other. In the midst of staring down at my yellow stream, I noticed that right next to me Tennessee Williams was also relieving himself. I looked over at him, and he realized that I had recognized him. He smiled and said, "You know, we will have to stop meeting like this." I laughed uncomfortably, and when we were both out of the toilet, I asked him how he liked the show. He said that he was very impressed by the level of the talent and that he loved the production.

FLYING WITH GUIDO PANZINI

Pat Harrington

It was 1957 and "The Tonight Show" was hosted by a droll guy named Jack Paar. A fairly good interviewer, he was affable and well-mannered. I used to watch the show occasionally, when there weren't any good movies at that time of night. His guests were usually there to plug their recent film or sometimes just to talk. A guy who supposedly was a famous Italian golfer named Guido Panzini appeared regularly on the show. He spoke with a heavy Italian accent and was very funny. It was sometime later that I found out that it was a put-on and that Panzini was in reality a comedian named Pat Harrington, Jr. It seems that Paar had seen Pat performing somewhere and had invited him on the show to do that character. It brought Pat instant visibility and he became well known. He went to Vegas and did very well, made a lot of money, moved to Los Angeles and bought a house in Bel Air. According to a mutual friend of ours, Greg Mullavey, who met him in my class, Pat decided he wanted to act, so he came to my class sometime around 1965. I had been teaching for about five years at the time.

Pat was very funny and everyone responded to him immediately. He studied with me for several years and became a good actor. Over the years he built up a very impressive résumé and ultimately did a television show called "One Day at a Time," which ran for several years. He appeared in over two hundred episodes and even wrote and directed a number of them.

Pat was a pilot and flew single-engine planes that he rented in Santa Monica. I told him that I had been flying with my cousin Lee and that I was crazy about it. He invited me to go up with him. He rented a low-wing single-engine airplane, a Mooney mark 5 that had a cruising speed of about two hundred and twenty-five miles an hour. I was really excited. After his pre-flight check I climbed into the cabin, sat in the co-pilot seat, fastened my seat belt and was excitedly looking forward to the takeoff.

I was enamored with flying, had been reading all the magazines about it, and whenever I could, I would join my cousin on a Saturday or Sunday for a few hours in the air. While I was living in Chicago and going to college, I took several flying lessons at a small local airport. Unfortunately, I got derailed by the responsibilities of school and never went far enough to solo. I had fantasies that while on a trip in a very large airplane, the pilots would become incapacitated and the flight attendants would ask the passengers if there was anyone who knew how to pilot an airplane. I would raise my hand and volunteer. They would then lead me to the cockpit and I would begin to take over, placing my headphones on so I could get help from the ground. I figured if I could drive a car, then this would be like driving a big eighteen-wheel truck. Driving is driving, I thought. Listening to the instructions from the ground and depending on whatever skills I had, I would successfully fly the plane and land it at the airport, making a skillful touchdown. I was a hero in my fantasies.

Pat had taken off with the expertise of a seasoned pilot, and we were in the air. He flew north over Santa Barbara and on into the Santa Inez Valley. He said he wanted to do a "touch and go" landing and takeoff at an airport there, so he communicated with the traffic controller at that small airport and was given permission to do a touch and go. Lee had never done anything like that, so it was a first for me. It was fun. We flew over the desert soon after that, and Pat looked over at me and said that he was really tired and wanted to take a nap. I thought he was kidding, but he crossed his arms, rested them on his chest, closed his eyes and said, "Take over, kid." We were up about five thousand feet. I checked all the instruments: the airspeed, the level flight indicator, the radio setting, and the throttle. I put both my hands firmly on the "stick," which was more like a cut-down steering wheel. I figured I should also check out the controls, so I banked right, putting some pressure on the rudder pedals, and the plane responded beautifully. I decided to turn to the left and reversed the procedure. I was on level flight at five thousand feet, so I pushed the throttle toward the instrument panel and got an immediate response from the engine. I pulled back the stick and began to climb to a higher altitude.

I was having the time of my life. Every time I did something I glanced over to check and see if Pat was really asleep. He seemed totally uninvolved, so I continued my adventure. I decided to become a fighter pilot who was attacking enemy ground installations, so I tilted the plane downward, never decreasing the engine speed, and pretended that I was firing the machine guns in the wing. I dropped down a couple of thousand feet, and after knocking out the enemy fortifications, I leveled off and came around for another go at them. I was really flying this plane and flying it well! After about fifteen minutes, Pat pretended to wake up. He smiled and said that I was a born pilot and should get my pilot's license. I asked him if he had really been asleep, and he smiled coyly. We landed safely. Unfortunately, I never got to fly with Guido Panzini again.

SHE'S AN ACTRESS—NO, SHE'S NOT!

Several years ago I was sitting in my office at my theater. Usually, either I am not there or I just let the answering machine field my calls, but on that day I was looking over a list of monologues that I wanted to assign to several of my students, when the phone rang, so I answered it. On the other end a very deep, and maybe a little raspy, voice asked if this was the Eric Morris Actors' Workshop. I replied that it was and that I, Eric, was the one speaking.

"I'm calling you about Anna Nicole Smith," the voice said.

"Yeah, so what do you want?" I responded.

"Well, you teach acting, don't you?"

"Yes, I do."

"Well, she's an actress," the man said.

Without taking a beat I responded, "No, she's not," and he hung up.

"THE SILENT SERVICE" HAD ITS FUNNY MOMENTS

When I got out of the army in December of 1956 and started pursuing my acting career, most of the parts I got were soldiers, sailors, or marines. I just couldn't get out of the military! I had been drafted right out of a show I was supposed to start rehearsing for, *My Three Angels,* which I had done in summer stock and which was scheduled to open in Palm Springs. I was to play the same part I had done in stock. It was the first acting job I had gotten after arriving in Hollywood, so I really resented being drafted, and I spent much of my military career bitching and moaning about having my acting career interrupted. Fortunately I did three plays at the Wharf Theatre in Monterey while at Fort Ord, and I wangled my way into being a disc jockey at the hospital radio station by telling them that I was a professional radio announcer in civilian life. Finally, after serving one year eleven months seventeen days and six hours, I received an honorable discharge. I could not, however, escape the military; for the first year of my reignited career I was never out of uniform!

Jack Lord

One show I was hired to do was a series called "The Silent Service," which was about the submarine service. I actually did a number of segments. The show was shot on a real submarine, the USS *Sawfish,* which was in the water in Long Beach, but tied to the dock. I played a variety of sailors in one or another segment where we were either under attack or in some other significant theatrical plot emergency.

I remember one show in particular: Jack Lord (who later became famous for "Hawaii Five-O") had just come to Hollywood from New York, where he had established a visible career. He was playing the captain of the submarine that had just suffered an attack from a Japanese airplane. He was on the bridge surveying the damage, and I came up to the bridge with a bucket supposedly filled with shrapnel caused by the bomb that had hit the sub. I said my line, which was, "Look, Captain, a whole bucketful," as I showed him the contents of the bucket. He looked at me and lost it. He began to laugh so hard that they had to stop the shooting. Sobey Martin, the director, a roly-poly middle-aged man with a pleasant personality, approached us and asked if there was a problem. Jack pulled himself together, and we got ready to shoot the scene again. I made my entrance on the bridge. Jack looked at me and lost it again! At that point I started to be insecure. Was it the way I looked, or was it the way I delivered the line? My hat was a little askew, so I straightened it, thinking that if I looked more like a sailor he wouldn't crack up when he looked at me. That was the fourth take, and those segments were to be shot in three or four days, so there wasn't time to screw around. On the fourth take, halfway through the line, I broke up. I couldn't stop laughing. They cut the scene. It did not appear in the show!

WHAT WOULD HAPPEN IF THERE WASN'T ANYTHING TO LEAN ON?

My agent's voice was filled with excitement as he told me that I got a lead in a two-part "Kraft Suspense Theatre," a television anthology show. As I said earlier, I was to play the part of Tippo, a Middle European assassin who comes to the United States with a partner to kill a high-ranking dignitary at a UN party. I was elated! It was something that I could sink my teeth into. Jan Merlin, my partner, had just come off a series called "Rough Riders." The rest of the cast included Hugh O'Brian, Barbara Rush (whom I knew from the Phil Silvers' days), Neil Hamilton, Harry Townes and a group of other actors whose faces were familiar.

O'Brian was well known for his role in "The Life and Legend of Wyatt Earp," a television series that ran for a period of time. He had also done a number of films and to his personal credit had very generously and charitably created an organization to help young kids grow and better themselves. In this show he played a cop who was assigned to the event and was the hero of the piece. I watched his work in a variety of scenes. In almost every one he found something to lean on. It could have been the corner of a desk or the back of a chair, or he would lean with folded arms against a wall. In every case he seized the opportunity to look relaxed and in control. At that time I had had a number of years of training and had also started my own teaching career, and I was familiar with all of the compensations that actors use to look relaxed and comfortable in a scene. Many years later I gave the phenomenon a name: "the limp-wristed school of acting." It is a way for actors to deal with their discomfort or tension by redirecting their behavior into what appears to be a state of relaxation and comfort. In O'Brian's case I don't think it was because he was tense or necessarily uncomfortable. I believe it had become a conditioned behavior that may have started out as a redirection but had become part of his acting demeanor. At this point I feel it is necessary to say that I have seen him do creditable work in other films.

On the fourth or fifth day of shooting I approached Jack Smight, the director of the piece, and said to him, "You know, if you shot a scene with O'Brian in an empty lot, you would be in trouble." He was puzzled by my statement and kept looking at me as I walked away.

SO ARE YOU A PORSCHE DEALER?

I live in the Hollywood hills. For a number of years my neighbor across the street was the famous mystery novelist Michael Connelly. For months we would smile and wave at each other, but we had never spoken. One time, not knowing who he was, I asked him what he did for a living and he told me that he was a writer. I smiled and told him that I too had written some books—not fiction but technical books about acting—and that I taught acting. He started to laugh and said that he had thought I was a Porsche dealer, since he saw me moving my three Porsches in and out of my garage. We had a good laugh, and he gave me one of his novels, *The Concrete Blonde.* I gave him *No Acting Please.* After a few years he moved away. Recently, I saw him here in the hills, because someone was doing a documentary on him and wanted to photograph the house where he had written one of his books. He told me that he was living in Florida now.

FROM BIG AND TALL TO SHORT AND SMALL

It was 1959, and I was fairly busy as an actor. I was cast in a number of 20th Century Fox pictures. They were small roles, but each had some substance. I worked with very big, legendary Hollywood directors, carryovers from the glory days of the motion-picture industry. I had a role as a soldier in *Rally 'Round the Flag, Boys!* which was directed by Leo McCarey and starred Paul Newman, Joanne Woodward and Tuesday Weld in one of her early roles. I played a military-police airman in *Holiday for Lovers,* directed by Henry Levin and starring Clifton Webb, Jane Wyman, Jill St John, Carol Lynley, Gary Crosby, and Gardner McKay in a small part. I was directed by Raoul Walsh in *A Private's Affair,* where I played a military-hospital orderly. After that, I was again a soldier opposite Dick Shawn, working as a radar specialist in *Wake Me When It's Over,* directed by Mervyn LeRoy. I had been discharged from the army just a year or two earlier, but, as I said above, it seemed that I couldn't escape being a soldier in films!

When I was doing *Holiday for Lovers,* Gardner McKay was one of the other soldiers in several scenes we were in together. He was a contract player at 20th, and, as was true for all the actors under contract, the studio threw him into almost every film that needed bodies. At that time a negotiation was going on with Gardner for him to have the leading role in a television series, "Adventures in Paradise," and he seemed embarrassed to be seen in this small uncredited role, so he hid behind me, bending his knees to make himself shorter so that he could not be seen. He did that whenever he could. If you were to watch the film, you would see me in a white military-police helmet, leading a group of airmen down the street, and if you looked closely, you might catch a glimpse of Gardner's head peeking just below my left shoulder. Gardner was strikingly handsome, looked a lot like Tyrone Power, but was inches taller. The series he was in ran for some years and many episodes. Sometime after that he gave up acting to become a playwright. He wrote a play, *Sea Marks,* and did scenes from it at the Actors Studio. That was the last time I saw him before he passed away.

WHICH EYE DID HE REALLY SEE WITH?

There are characters and there are characters. In my sixty plus years in this business I have crossed paths with many unforgettable characters. One of them was an actor named Clegg Hoyt. Running into him on the street was itself an experience. He weighed about two hundred and fifty pounds and was about five feet ten inches tall. His sandy gray hair was always clipped short, his face was bright red, and he was always perspiring and out of breath, as if he had just run up a flight of stairs. He had a voice like a foghorn with laryngitis. He spoke louder than anybody else around him, but because he was always ready with a big-tooth smile, people accepted and liked him. He was a character actor and had a large résumé of work in films. He was the kind of actor you see and recognize but whose name you really do not know, someone for whom you might say, "Oh there's that guy, the actor, you know, the one we see in movies."

Every day I would run down the hill to Schwab's Pharmacy for breakfast. If one wonders why actors hang out in various places, I have a theory about that: Actors are lonely and always waiting for their agent to call them with an audition to go to. So hanging out with their own kind is what you might call comforting. At any rate Clegg was one of those actors who hung out at Schwab's. He had a special attribute, a glass eye. Sometimes it was a regular glass eye matching the other real eye, but quite often it was a glass eye that had an American flag covering most of its surface. At first, it was unnerving to see one eye looking at you and the other with a flag instead of an eye; however, after a while you got used to it and treated it as you would a normal part of a person's body.

One evening I dropped into the restaurant for a quick bite, and there was Clegg eating some soup. He was alone at the large booth the group always sat at, so I joined him. We spoke for a while about what actors talk about—working. In the middle of a sentence his glass eye fell out and into the soup. There I was, staring at an open eye socket without an eye in it. Without missing a beat Clegg looked at the eye in the soup and said, "It's very protective of me, and so it's in there checking out the soup to see if it's alright for me to eat." I was so shocked I couldn't respond, laugh, gasp, or do whatever one does in such an unusual situation. He proceeded to extricate the eye from the soup, wiped it off and replaced it into its socket. I had lost my appetite by that time, so I made some lame excuse as to why I had dropped in to begin with, and I courteously made an exit.

THE TALLEST NINE-YEAR-OLD BOY IN TOWN

Hampton Fancher

The Tallest Nine-Year-Old Boy in Town was the name of a short play I wrote, which we performed at the Actors Studio in Hollywood. It was about Hampton Fancher, one of my earliest students, who started working with me in 1962 or '63 and became a close friend. Hampton, whom I have talked about earlier in this book, was one of those people who could have been the subject of a *Readers Digest* article entitled "One of the Most Unforgettable Characters," a series that appeared regularly in that magazine. Very colorful and totally unpredictable, he was a very talented actor, who had done a number of films and television shows. At the time he started working with me he was living with Joan Blackman, also a working actress, who had had an impressive early career. Hampton brought Joan to my class, and we worked together for some time.

Women loved Hampton. They were attracted to him as flies to honey, and he knew exactly how to handle them. It was a talent that I admired and also envied. In addition, I have always been very impressed with the fact that almost every woman he has ever been involved with remained his friend after their romance ended. While he was working with me and after his relationship to Joan ended, he met and married Sue Lyon, the actress who played Lolita in the film of the same name. He also brought her to my class. She was very talented and courageously did characters there that were quite a stretch for her. After that relationship ended, Hampton got involved and lived with Teri Garr, who also studied with me. She came to my class directly off a television dance show and never did any comedy scenes in class but instead always did serious characters and seemed attracted to them.

I'm not sure about the timeline, but at some point Hampton began writing and moved from acting into writing. He lived in a small, charming house in Topanga Canyon, I believe for many years. I visited him several times there, and I must say that Topanga Canyon attracts a very special kind of person—artists, writers, or hippies, many of whom use their backyards to grow marijuana. The village, which hosts a group of grocery stores and a couple of hardware establishments, attracts inhabitants who seem to look as though they came out of a different century. It was there that, as I mentioned before, Hampton wrote some screenplays, among them *Blade Runner,* which became a legendary film that has had a history of influencing science-fiction movies up to the present time.

While living in the canyon he was seriously troubled by a rat. Usually rats live in small families, but this seemed to be a single rat that staked out his house. Every time Hampton sat down to write or at night when he was trying to sleep, he heard scratching on the wall and in the ceiling. It was as if the rat knew exactly how to irritate him. It would rhythmically scratch in the wall nearest to where Hampton was writing and at night exactly above his bed. When he would leave the house to go shopping or take a walk, he would return to find that things he had left on a table were missing—all kinds of things: dental floss, matchbooks, and even a package of condoms. What began as an irritation grew into a competitive battle between him and the rat. He bought rat traps, the kind that when sprung would break the rat's neck or spine. He was angry and filled with the need to destroy that rat. He put cheese as bait on the trap, but when he investigated the trap, hoping to see a dead rat, he only found the cheese missing and the trap intact. He tried tying the cheese so that the rat would have a difficult time getting it away from there and would hopefully spring the trap, but that didn't work either. He had heard that rats could not resist peanut butter, so he wrapped the cheese in peanut butter, only to discover that the rat had licked the peanut butter off the cheese and had not sprung the trap. This whole battle took over his life. He found that, instead of being able to write, he used the time to devise new strategies to kill that rat. At night he pounded on the ceiling with the handle of a broom, and the rat responded by scratching back at the same point. He contemplated calling an exterminator but figured that the rat would also outsmart him. It elevated into a contest between man and beast! He desperately needed to sleep and to be able to write.

A neighbor down the canyon was moving back East and had a cat that he didn't want to abandon, so Hampton seized on the opportunity to take the cat. He made friends with it, feeding it and creating a relationship with it, since he saw this as his salvation. For a day or two the scratching stopped and he felt victorious in this war between him and the rat. On the third day, however, the scratching began again with renewed vigor. He sat the cat down and had a long conversation with it, asking for help in catching the rat. He was so desperate he actually believed that the cat would understand his pleas. Days went by and the rat's attack escalated. At one point Hampton thought he heard a ruckus behind the wall, and he figured that the cat had gotten the rat and it would finally be over. The next day, however, the cat had disappeared and the rat was still scratching! He figured that if he couldn't kill the rat with traps, maybe he could catch it. He went to a pet store and bought a small cage with a trap door that would close as the rat entered the cage. He filled it with all kinds of delectable goodies—cheese, meat, peanut butter—placed it in the center of the living-room floor, and left the house, slamming the door so the rat would know that he had left! When he returned, the rat was in the cage, frantically scurrying around looking for an exit. Hampton picked up the cage, set it on the table and viewed the rat as it attempted to find freedom. This was a nine-inch gray rat with long blackish hair growing from its pimpled skin and a tail as long as its body. When Hampton and the rat made eye contact, it was as if the vanquished eyed the victor with disgust. This was one of those memorable moments when one could really celebrate victory and assert man's superiority over the rest of the animal kingdom. It was a time to feel relieved at the end of a long battle.

The question was what to do with the rat. Should he kill it? drown it? If he let it go, it would probably do the same thing to someone else. He decided to turn it loose at a restaurant down the road where he had had some difficulty with the owners at one time.

It was one of those health-food restaurants, owned by a guy who wore a turban and a long white robe and ministered by young girls also dressed in the same way. Hampton had been asked to leave because he had been sitting there for too long after finishing his meal. So one night after the restaurant was closed, he took the rat cage, pried the back door of the restaurant open, and released the rat, disposing of the cage in a clump of bushes on the way back to his house. With great relief he went to bed and had a good night's sleep. For a couple of days everything was quiet, and he was able to reinvest in his writing.

He was sitting on the couch with a beer and a cigarette when he heard scratching behind the same wall. Oh my God! He leapt to his feet and screamed at the wall. The rat had followed him home! The battle was renewed and went on for a couple of weeks, until one day, on his way back from lunch, he saw the skin and tail of a fully eaten rat hanging from one of the trees surrounding his house. He figured that one of the owls that frequented the neighborhood had gotten the rat and had a good meal. He was able to finish his screenplay in peace!

Hampton moved to New York at some point and while there continued to write and do some teaching. He had been contracted to write a screenplay, but for whatever reason he was taking more time to deliver the property to the producers than they were expecting, so they showed up at his apartment building, which had a uniformed doorman, and asked to be announced to "Happen Faster"!

A FUNNY MAN WHO DID SOME NOT SO FUNNY THINGS

Joy Morris was my former wife. She had moved to Los Angeles in the summer of 1972 and had found a job at a famous Hollywood restaurant called Yamashiro. Yamashiro sits on top of a hill in the heart of Hollywood and is known for its breathtaking, panoramic view of Los Angeles. Inside the palace itself you find a lovely Japanese garden and architecture that is a work of art. As you drive up a driveway that winds its way to the top, alongside the restaurant are apartments and guesthouses. The entire property is family owned by T. Y. Glover. She fell in love with the place instantly and took a job as an accountant, secretary, and apartment manager, basically doing whatever was needed in the office, something she wormed her way into by professing to have had experience. The truth was that she had had very little, but she learns quickly and knew she could do the job.

We were together when she worked at Yamashiro, and I remember an experience she had there about two weeks after she arrived. As far as my memory serves me, I will try to recount it exactly as she told it to me at the time:

Richard Pryor

One day, "a young black man walked in. The other three people who worked in the office had not yet arrived, and so I was alone. He walked over to the desk and handed me a check. I looked up, smiled sweetly and asked, 'What is this for?'

"He politely replied, 'It's for the broken down door in my house.'

"'Which house is it?' I asked."

(There were three guesthouses on the property; one was called the Monkey House, another was the Tea House, while the third didn't have a specific name or at least not one that I can recall. It was just the corner guesthouse.)

"'Just tell them it's Pryor's house. They'll understand.'

"'Okay,' I said, 'and you are?'

"He stood for a moment, looked at me kind of funny, grinned, then sauntered back over to where I was sitting at my desk. He began spelling his full name while I wrote it down, R-I-C-H-A-R-D P-R-Y-O-R. Once I'd written it down I took his check and the note and set them aside.

"'Thank you,' I said. 'I'll give the check to Sharon when she comes in to work.' (Sharon also worked the desk and usually took care of matters that concerned the apartments.) 'We'll get your door repaired ASAP,' I assured him.

"Richard stood there for a minute still staring at me with a sly grin on his face, as though he wanted to say something, but he just smiled and said, 'Thanks.'

"'You're welcome,' I said.

"Then, before he walked away, he asked, 'And you are?'

"'Joy,' I told him.

"He headed for the door but a second later came back and peeked inside. 'By the way,' he said, 'the door needs to be replaced, not repaired.'

"'Are you sure it can't be fixed?' I asked.

"'Absolutely,' he replied, laughing as he spoke.

"'Fine, I'll tell Sharon to take a look at it.'

"'Thanks, Joy.'

"'You're welcome, Richard. Thanks for letting us know,' I responded in my nice receptionist manner.

"When Sharon came to work, I handed her the check and told her what had happened. She looked at me astonished and asked, 'You don't know who Richard Pryor is?'

"'No,' I said. 'Is he somebody I should know?'

"'He's probably the most famous comedian of this time right now.'

"I was completely embarrassed. I couldn't believe I had asked him who he was and to spell his name. Sharon explained the situation to me. Richard and his girlfriend lived in one of the houses on the hill. Frequently, they would get into some pretty bad ruckuses. Richard would go out, get drunk or stay out all night, and then come home, but his girlfriend wouldn't let him in, and so he would just break the door down. Each time he did it he would come in with a check and have the door paid for and replaced. Once, his girlfriend was so angry with him she actually placed his Porsche on the top of the hill and let it roll down and crash.

"Sharon also told me, just in case someone from the Tea House came, that his name was Pernell Roberts and to pretend that I knew him." (Pernell was a very famous TV star at the time. He was one of the three sons on the series "Bonanza.")

MERVYN LEROY'S GREAT IDEA

Mervyn LeRoy was a very successful and popular director, who directed *Mister Roberts, Quo Vadis, Gypsy, A Majority of One, The Devil at 4 O'Clock, Wake Me When It's Over, The FBI Story,* and numerous others. I mentioned earlier that I had appeared in

Wake Me When It's Over. I had a scene with Dick Shawn, where I played an airman at a computer. However, that is not the story.

My brother Ed Morris was under contract to Columbia at the time. Somehow LeRoy had heard some good things about his writing, so he contacted him and invited him for lunch at the commissary at 20th Century Fox. I remember that my brother was very excited by the invitation. He dressed for the occasion and met with Mervyn LeRoy in the commissary. After the usual introductions and background sharing, LeRoy pursed his lips, smiled through them, and announced that he had an incredible title for a film that he would like my brother Ed to write. He really played the moment, behaving as if he had discovered the cure for cancer. Finally he blurted out the title: *Cowboys and Indians.* Ed just sat there speechless and totally taken aback by LeRoy's excitement. At first he thought it was a joke, so he laughed, which LeRoy did not appreciate at all. When Ed saw his response, he asked him if he was indeed serious about this. LeRoy turned red and started to stutter. He was so angry he couldn't get a whole sentence past his lips. At that point, my brother, being the salty prick that he was, entirely impatient with other people's inadequacies, stood up from the table and looked directly at LeRoy. "Mr. LeRoy," he said, "you are a fucking moron," and he left.

WHO ARE YOU?

Alejandro Rey was a South American actor who did a number of films and most notably had a costarring role in "The Flying Nun" with Sally Field. He studied with me for some time, and one evening while doing a monologue onstage, he related this humorous story:

He was dining at a hotel in Rome when the waiter approached him and asked, "Are you who I think I think you are?"

To which Alejandro responded, "Who do you think you think I am?"

I don't remember whether the waiter replied and what he said if he did.

MINE IS BIGGER THAN YOURS

Milton Berle

This story has been circulating around Hollywood for years, and I have recently heard it again for the third or fourth time. The content differs slightly with every storyteller, but the basic story remains the same. It seems that Milton Berle was known for having a huge penis—or he had possibly made that known. For quite some time it was a topic of conversation and humor at the Friars Club in Beverly Hills, to which he belonged and where many famous actors and comics congregated to play cards and schmooze. Berle enjoyed the comedy and laughter stimulated by the subject. Then Fess Parker joined the club and somehow made it known that he too had an oversized tool. The story about Berle and Parker went back and forth at the club for some time. Everyone was very involved in the competitiveness between them. In fact they became quite serious about the contest, but of course it was just words and accusations flying around the room. Finally, one of the members suggested that they show their wares, and everyone would place bets on his favorite.

The big night arrived. The crowd gathered in the locker room, and both men stood facing each other like two gunfighters in the Old West. Parker was first to expose his stuff, and just about the time when Berle was going to do the same, Buddy Hackett screamed from the other side of the room, "Milton, just pull out enough to win the bet!"

THE IRREVERENT BETTE DAVIS

A number of years ago I was sitting in a booth at Schwab's Pharmacy on Sunset Boulevard. At the table were Bette Davis in her declining years; Huntz Hall, one of the original East Side Kids; Jack Ackerman, a music producer; and myself. Bette was very verbal and extremely opinionated, and every third or fourth word out of her mouth was fuck this or that or him or her. I had always thought of her as a fine actress, and I was extremely amused by her openness and profanity.

Bette Davis

Besides having a sailor's foul mouth she spoke many times with either cruel or irreverent humor. While visiting a Catholic church (possibly doing research for a film), she saw a priest heading up the aisle towards her dressed in a ceremonious robe and swinging a brass vessel that was burning incense and emitting white smoke as it swung from side to side. She stopped, looked at the priest, and said, "I like your robe, but your purse is on fire!"

THE BULBOUS-NOSED DRUNK

W.C. Fields was a very famous actor and comic in the thirties and early forties. A notorious drunk, while strolling down the street one day, he was approached by an irate overweight, middle-aged woman who disgustingly told him that he was an awful drunk. He took a moment to appraise the whole situation and then said, "That's right lady, I'm drunk, and tomorrow I'll be sober; but you will always be ugly," and he strolled away.

Fields was very competitive with Charlie Chaplin, who was always touted as the best actor of that period. Fields resented the comparison and at every opportunity would make some critical comment about Chaplin. One of his friends took him to see one of Chaplin's movies, and on exiting the theater Fields said, "That guy is not an actor; he is a fucking ballet dancer!"

When he was approached by an accountant hired to prepare his income taxes, he was asked if he invested his money wisely, and if so in what.

"Why yes," he replied, "I invest all my money in houses and lots."

"Houses and lots?"

"Yes, whorehouses and lots of whisky!"

THE BLOND WITH BIG TITS AND A DEEP VOICE

Mae West was also an interesting character of that same period, the late thirties and early forties, and she was known for her wit and sexual innuendos. She had platinum blond hair down to her shoulders and breasts so large that they were the first part of her anatomy that walked through the door. Her voice and style of delivery were uniquely hers, and she used to address most men with "Hey there, big boy." In one case, in either a show or a film, she delivered a variant of that great line that was almost a signature line for her: A man enters the scene, she looks at him all the way down to his crotch and says, "Hey there, big boy, is that a pickle in your pocket or are you happy to see me?"

THE SON OF GOD ON THE CROSS

This is one of those stories that have circulated around Hollywood for almost as long as I have been here. Even if it never happened, it is quite amusing. It was one of those biblical productions that involve the crucifixion of Christ. The scene takes place at the foot of the cross. A group of actors dressed in period costumes were standing there looking up at Jesus. As the story goes, the director went up to John Wayne, who was playing one of the parts, and said to him, "Look, Duke, this is the son of God. Please, with awe!"

The director called action. Wayne approached the cross, looked up at the actor doing Jesus, and in a very audible voice uttered a very emotional "aww!"

DIRECTOR MICHAEL CURTIZ AND THE WILLING EXTRA

Michael Curtiz was a director of well over a hundred films and an Oscar winner with many more nominations. Although he was Hungarian, he did almost all of his films in America. They include some of the most famous classic films that have ever come out of Hollywood: *Mildred Pierce* with Joan Crawford, *Casablanca* with

Ingrid Bergman and Humphrey Bogart, *Yankee Doodle Dandy, White Christmas,* and many others.

On one of his films he seduced a pretty young extra into giving him a blow job. He sequestered himself behind the wall of a set, found a comfortable chair, and was in the midst of receiving fellatio, when some of the crew members, who knew what was going on, proceeded to roll away the wall of that set and totally exposed the action taking place. Everyone there could see what was happening. When Curtiz became aware that he was totally exposed, he jumped up, exclaiming with the most shocking expression, "Hey, what are you doing? Stop that! Get away from me!" People talked about it for years afterwards.

Curtiz had an accent, and quite often his English lacked certain colloquialisms. On one occasion he asked the property master to get him a "poodle." The property master brought him a small dog, only to find out that what Curtiz had actually wanted was a *puddle* of water! In another movie, *Cabin in the Cotton,* the screenwriter had described the characters in the scene as a bunch of "peckerwoods," so Curtiz asked the actors to behave like woodpeckers!

HEY, PAY ATTENTION TO THE PASTA AND LET ME DO MY JOB

James Wong Howe was a legendary Academy Award-winning cinematographer, who was the director of photography on one hundred and thirty-nine films, including *Hud, The Molly Maguires; Funny Lady; The Heart is a Lonely Hunter; Hombre; The Last Angry Man; This Property Is Condemned; Bell, Book, and Candle,* and so on. He also directed seven films. He was attending the opening of a friend's Italian restaurant somewhere in the Valley, when all of the owners and guests were summoned outside in front of the restaurant for a group picture. They were all positioned by the photographer, one of those guys who make a living shooting proms, banquets, bar mitzvahs, weddings, and other family events. He was using a Speed Graphic plate camera, and just when he was ready to take the picture, James Wong Howe said to him that if he moved back one foot he would get a better frame line, and if he shot the picture from a different angle the light would be better.

The photographer stepped out from behind the camera, walked up to Howe and said, "Look, buddy, you pay attention to the pasta and let me do my job!"

IT'S GRANNY GOOSE, WHO ELSE?

Philip Carey

A number of years ago there was a commercial on television featuring an actor named Philip Carey, a tall, handsome man who played a range of parts, including westerns. The commercial was a takeoff on the movie *The Treasure of the Sierra Madre,* particularly the scene where the Mexican bandits encounter Humphrey Bogart.

The dialogue was similar in the commercial: Carey was stopped by the four Mexican bandits, who said (in a Mexican accent), "Hey, you, what's your name?"

Sitting straight up on his horse, Carey responded, "I'm Granny Goose."

At that point the bandits pointed to Carey's saddlebag, asking, "What's in the bag, Goose?"

Reaching into it, Carey took out a bag of Granny Goose potato chips and replied, "Why, these are Granny Goose potato chips, the finest chips made," or something of that nature.

That was the commercial. Unfortunately, as the story goes, every time Carey was seen in an airport or other places, kids would point to him and scream, "There's Granny Goose!" I have no idea how that affected his acting career, but I'm sure it took a while for him to shed the Granny Goose image.

SONNY TUFTS…SONNY TUFTS… SONNY TUFTS?

He was a tall, blond, and very good-looking guy, who appeared in a number of films in the late forties and early fifties. He was not a bad actor, nor was he a very good one either. He was affable,

Sonny Tufts

pleasant to look at, with a sonorous voice. A lot of things can happen in the course of an actor's career, some of them damaging unfortunately. In this case it came from an impulsive accident. Joan Bennett was announcing the show for the following week on "The Lux Radio Theater," a radio anthology program that Lux soap sponsored. There was a different show each week, and one of its actors would always announce the show for the following week. Joan started by saying something like, "Next week's show is 'The House of the Seven Gables' and will feature George Brent, Agnes Moorehead, Vincent Price, and...*Sonny Tufts???*" She was obviously reading from a paper, and when she read Tufts' name, she was so shocked and taken aback by his appearing alongside those venerable actors that she sounded dumbfounded. It carried over the airwaves and created a phenomenon that lasted years and ruined Sonny's career. It became a catch phrase that people in the industry would use when expressing incredulity, surprise or criticism: SONNY TUFTS???

HE WAS REALLY A YANKEE DOODLE DANDY

There are many stories about James Cagney. He was a legendary actor, having done scores of films. He sang, danced, acted, and played a wide variety of characters. He went from being a song-and-dance man in *Yankee Doodle Dandy* to playing vicious gangsters, killers and everything in between. He was imitated by many mimics, who most always would start their imitation by saying, "You dirty rat..." When he was awarded a Lifetime Achievement Award, he took the mike, and one of the first things he said was, "I never said you dirty rat...I never said that!"

He grew up in a Jewish neighborhood, had many Jewish friends, and was frequently invited to a fine Jewish dinner, especially on high holidays. As a result, he learned to understand and speak Yiddish fluently. As the story goes—and this is one that has been passed down in Hollywood folklore—he was in the office with the two Warner brothers, who were speaking to each other in Yiddish about trying to negotiate his contract, making him a lower offer and getting him to sign for less money than he wanted. Cagney just sat there listening. When they were finished and returned to speaking English, Cagney told them in fluent Yiddish that they couldn't begin to hustle him into a lower salary and that if they insisted he would move to another studio. Well, can you imagine their shock at hearing Cagney respond to them in their own language?

Cagney had a very long career. Towards the end of it he started to paint, as many actors and some directors have done. As the story goes, while working on his last film, he walked out of the dark soundstage into the beautiful Southern California sun, looked up at the blue sky, and said, "I'm done," thus ending his acting career.

IS IT REALLY TOUGH, EDDIE?

Stories circulate around Hollywood for decades and become part of the folklore. Every once in a while one of those stories will invade my brain and make me laugh, and if I'm with a group of people, or with just one other person, my response seems to come from nowhere and creates raised eyebrows. This is one of those stories that I have heard. It is about Edmund Gwenn, an English actor who worked in American films for many years. He was a small man with a twinkle in his eyes, and whenever he appeared on screen, he lit it up with a compelling inner life. He was a curmudgeon, a character with a kind of magnetism that you just had to watch. He did scores of films, creating all sorts of characters, from an archbishop to a hired killer. His most famous performance was as Kris Kringle (Santa Claus) in *Miracle on 34th Street,* with Maureen O'Hara, John Payne, and Natalie Wood as a young child. The film airs every Christmas and has become a classic, just like *It's a Wonderful Life*.

As I have heard the story, Edmund Gwenn was dying at the Motion Picture Country Home, a place where actors take up residence in their later or declining years. He was in bed, being visited by an old friend, who stood by his bedside. Gwenn was in pain and in the process of dying, when his friend took his hand and said, "Is it really tough, Eddie?" to which Gwenn in a whisper responded,

"Not as tough as playing comedy," which in itself might not impact the average person, but if you are an actor, that response is totally understandable and contains both pathos and humor.

THAT CHECK WILL NEVER BE CASHED

Years ago it was a common practice for famous movie stars to pay for their purchases with a check—mostly small purchases, such as gasoline, groceries, and so on. The actors knew that the checks would never reach the bank but would end up on the wall of each business in a frame, because the store owner would proudly display each check as evidence of a personal connection with a big movie star and would even at times boast that that star was a regular customer and even a friend.

PRANKS AND MISCHIEF IN HOLLYWOOD

The following stories are humorous, to say the least. I was a witness to two of them, while the others were related to me by a person who was involved in the prank.

OK, IT STINKS

I was working on a television show, where I had a decent role, but I truly cannot remember what show it was. Stanley Clements was appearing in the same episode. He had a habit of coming up to an actor who had just finished a shot; with a big smile and his fingers configured in an OK sign, he would look right into that actor's eyes, say, "Stinks!" and walk away. At that time in my career I was more than a little insecure about my work, and when he did it to me, I took it seriously. Realizing that I was affected by his humorous gesture, he approached me, put his arms around me, and told me he was only kidding.

TIE A RED RIBBON AROUND IT

I was the associate producer on a film that was being directed by Michael Campus. I believe it was his first film. Titled *Survival,* it starred Barry Sullivan, Anne Francis, Sheree North, and several other recognizable name actors. I don't remember how I had gotten the job, but I think Michael had visited my class a couple of times and felt that I would be an asset to the film.

Whenever I worked on the other side of the camera, it was my habit to suggest or bring in my students to take part in or audition for the project. I had done a few projects for Roger and Gene Corman and had been able to get a number of my students hired on those. During a casting session for the Michael Campus film, Michael Green came in to read for one of the roles. Michael was an actor in my class and a very close friend of Hampton Fancher, who I believe had brought him into the class. Michael's picture appears on the cover of my second book, *Being & Doing*.

We were auditioning people in my theater, and besides the director, several other people involved in the project were sitting in the first row, including the director's fiancée. Michael came into the room, shook hands with everyone, looked at the script he was going to read from, and proceeded to drop his pants. Since he wasn't wearing any underwear, his genitals were completely exposed. On his flaccid penis was tied a red ribbon in a neat bow. He then proceeded to read the lines, but at that moment everyone was too shocked to listen to his words. He finished the monologue, lifted his trousers back up, zipped them up, thanked everyone and left. We all sat there speechless, not knowing how to respond. I was the one who was the most embarrassed, since I had brought him in. I apologized and explained to everyone that I didn't understand what had just occurred and that Michael had never exhibited that kind of behavior before.

Michael has now retired from acting and has a ranch in Hawaii. He loves working the land and is completing a novel. I am occasionally in contact with him, and to this day I don't understand why he did what he did at that audition, even though I know that he has a strange sense of humor and is prone to playing pranks or doing outrageous things. It is part of his charming personality.

DO IT LIKE THE DUKE

This story was actually told to me by Michael Green. I will recount it in his own words.

"I was about to begin filming on the series 'The Dakotas' about four federal marshals in the 1880s. I was cast as one of the leads, Vance Porter, US Marshal. In the Warner Bros. costume department, scarcely a week after a horrific bicycle accident, the scabs covering my back were getting horrified looks and lots of sympathy. Seepage from the wounds discolored my T-shirt. I tried on wool shirts and pants with no complaint, adding dusters and heavy jackets. Willy the boot maker was summoned to accommodate my size-fifteen feet. They made me three pairs of rough-outs with small heels so I wouldn't tower over the other three marshals, played by Chad Everett, Jack Elam, and Larry Ward.

"Contrary to what I told the producers, I knew very little about horses. They assigned me a big gelding, assuring me that he was gentle, and I got one of the Eppers boys, from the famous stuntmen family, as my double. Tony saw right away that I didn't know shit and patiently worked long hours with me until I was comfortable on the beast. On the back lot one day, while he was teaching me how to saddle and harness my horse, I commented on how lucky I was to have someone from that legendary family on my team.

"'You have to take a fall in the second show, Mike. Don't worry! I'll make you look good,' he told me.

"'Show me how you do it,' I said.

"He was reluctant.

"'Come on Tony, please,' I insisted. 'It'll help me make my ride up to the pit look good.'

"After cautioning me not to try it, he got on his horse, rode back fifty yards, then barreled up to the edge of the sandpit and flung himself off into the sand, rolling over and continuing to roll when he hit the sand. He then jumped up as if getting up from a nap.

"The sandpit was camouflaged to look like the hard earth surrounding it. If you missed it you'd be sorry. The technique was to fall off the horse backwards, spin around and land on your side while rolling to absorb the shock. I practiced it a number of times when Tony wasn't around.

"The first show went smoothly. Lee Sholem directed the second show. His nickname, 'Roll 'em Sholem,' represented his style: to work as fast as possible, thereby endearing himself to the studio executives. After the first take Roll 'em would yell, 'Cut! Print!' with his back to the set on his way to the next setup. Unnecessary delays were frowned upon as unprofessional. I thought Sholem was a kiss ass, and I didn't have much respect for him. When it came time for my stunt, he directed me to gallop right up to the camera and continue on by. Tony would take over after that and do the actual fall. 'Roger that, Lee,' I said.

"The camera was on the ground in front of the sandpit. The director yelled, 'Action!' I came at a pretty good clip, let go of the reins just in front of the camera, kicked my feet out of the stirrups, threw my hands in the air, screamed, rolled off the horse, and spun around just as Tony had done. I lay there motionless. There was a hush.

"'Jesus Christ,' Sholem hissed. He looked around. 'Where's Tony? Get me Tony.'

"'Maybe you'd better call a doctor,' someone said.

"That probably hadn't occurred to Roll 'em. He was focused on getting on to the next shot.

"'He's not moving,' someone else said.

"After a few minutes a doctor from one of the films shooting on the lot appeared. He reached for my pulse. I heard Sholem on the phone with my benefactor, Bill Orr, Jack Warner's son-in-law, who was also head of TV production.

"'His pulse is normal,' the doctor said.

"I popped up dramatically and responded, 'You're fucking right it is,' and then, looking at the cameraman, I asked, 'Shall we try it again?'

"Sholem was livid. 'You son-of-a-bitch, you son-of-a-bitch,' was all he could say.

"Bill Orr sent a message that he wanted to see me at lunchtime.

"'Why do you want to pull a stunt like that, Mike?' he asked. I shrugged. 'John Wayne would never pull a stunt like that…it's unprofessional,' he continued. 'Be smart! Do it like the Duke, Mike.'

"'Bill, I saved a whole setup by doing the stunt myself.'

"'Suppose you would have hurt yourself, then what?'

"'That's what I'm saying. The first thing Sholem asked for was the stuntman.'

"'You've got a great look. Don't screw it up. You're just getting started.'

"'I'm sorry, Bill. I'll be cool.' I hustled back to the set.
"'Don't try a trick like that again,' Sholem ordered.
"'Saved you a setup, boss,' I responded with a smile."

WHERE'S THE POOP?

An actor friend of mine told me this one: He was working as a grip on a film that was being shot in the desert. As is customary when productions are on location, there were trailers replete with dressing-room toilets and a place to sit or lie down. The scene that was being filmed, however, was taking place half a mile away from those trailers. As it happens, one of the production crew had to move his bowels. He excused himself, found a pretty large desert bush away from the cameras, pulled down his pants, and made ready to poop. A couple of the other grips carefully followed him, snuck up behind him, and extended a shovel directly under his anus. He proceeded to having a very satisfying and very large elimination, which was all caught by the shovel under him. Before he rose up from his pooping position, the other grips took off with his enormously large stool contribution and disappeared. When he turned around to view his poop, it wasn't there! He just stood there for several minutes looking at the ground and finally started to circle the immediate area. The look on his face was worth all the trouble the others had gone through. They laughed until their sides ached.

PROMISES, PROMISES, AND LIES

The other day I was having lunch with an old friend and former student—and when I say former I mean that he studied with me in the mid-sixties. Tony Russell, a man for all seasons, is an actor, comedian, singer and musician. He is terrific in all of those areas. Every time we get together I leave the table with a stomach ache from laughing so hard. He rattles off jokes like a machine gun. Each successive gag tops the previous one. I have gone to see him perform in various places and on a number of occasions. Watching him sit at the piano and sing is a treat, since he is a practiced pianist and can accompany himself while singing a large variety of songs. His film career has been steady in the last several years. He was also a regular on a television show, "Life with Bonnie" starring Bonnie Hunt. We were enjoying our lunch, trading jokes, when he told me this bizarre story that happened sometime in the early seventies:

Tony Russell

He was the house MC at Ye Little Club in Beverly Hills, where he would introduce singers, comedians and other types of entertainers. It was a cabaret kind of place that served as a showcase for up-and-coming performers. People such as Joan Rivers and others who were near the beginning of their careers appeared there. It was about the time Johnny Carson came to California and had a late-night television show. Being on that show was almost a guarantee of getting an incredible start in one's career, so every comic and singer wanted that exposure.

On that particular evening McLean Stevenson came into the club with two beautiful young women, one on each arm. They sat down at a table close to the stage, while Tony was doing his act. He immediately recognized Stevenson and pumped up his presentation. He was hot as a firecracker and got a lot of laughs and spontaneous applause. When he finished his act, Stevenson came up to him and told him that he was great.

"I have been sent down to look you over for the Carson show," he added. Following that with a wink, he continued, "You are in, Tony. You will appear on 'The Tonight Show.' Just call the network to set up the date of your appearance."

Tony was ecstatic and couldn't sleep a wink that night. He got out of bed around five in the morning, loaded up on coffee, and watched the clock, waiting for 9:00 A.M. to arrive. He kept thinking that time moves at a snail's pace when you are waiting for it to pass. Finally, when the minute hand hit twelve, he lifted the phone and called the network, asking to speak to the office of the Carson show. When they connected him to a gruff-voiced guy who seemed to have gotten up on the wrong side of the bed, Tony informed him that he was calling to schedule his appearance on the show.

There was an uncomfortably long silence, and then the gravel voice on the other end asked, "Who are you?" Tony told him what

Stevenson had said, that he had been sent down to the club to watch Tony, that Tony was definitely on the show, and that he should call for scheduling.

"Listen, I don't know who you are," the voice said. "We never sent anyone to look you over and you are not on this show."

The sound of the phone hitting its base was like a bomb going off in Tony's ear. It seemed like five minutes before he could put the phone down. He felt numb and in a swirling fog, and he couldn't assemble the components of the conversation. It was as if he was remembering every fourth word that gravel voice had said to him. It took a long time for him to get over that experience, and to this day he is confused about why Stevenson would have done something like that. I told him that I thought he was grandstanding for the girls he had come in with.

HOLLYWOOD FOLKLORE, RUMORS AND HEARSAY

For many years rumors and stories have populated Hollywood. They get passed from person to person, some so outrageous that they challenge belief. There are, however, many things one hears over and over from a variety of sources that make you think that where there is smoke there must be fire! The following stories have been floating around for decades, and I believe that they should be reported.

IN A STUDIO MOGUL'S OFFICE

Judy Garland was under contract to MGM, which Louis B. Mayer was running at the time. The rumor floated around that he would call Judy into his office to perform sexual favors for him. She was a teenager at the time. Her mother knew what was going on but was too afraid to rock the boat, so nothing was done about it. One then must wonder why Judy was so troubled for most of her life!

BE CAREFUL WHAT YOU SHOVE UP YOUR ANUS

A number of years ago there was a fad circulating in Hollywood—maybe in other places too. It concerned a little animal called a gerbil and what guys were doing with it. In order to have a sexual experience they were inserting it into their anus and allowing it to run around inside their bodies. The point was to have the gerbil stimulate the prostate, which excited the penis and supposedly sent pleasurable sensations into and through the genitals. It seemed to catch on, and many were doing it. As the story goes, a famous actor got one of those little rodents stuck somewhere inside his bowel and couldn't get it out. He was taken to the hospital with a paper bag over his head so as not to be recognized, and he had the poor thing taken out of his body. The question is: Was it considered cruelty to animals or did the guy get what he deserved?

ON THE SET OF THE MOVIE *GIANT*

A scene that included James Dean was being filmed on the porch of the mansion where Rock Hudson and Elizabeth Taylor lived in the movie *Giant.* The scene was shot over and over because Dean kept blowing lines and was unable to function. Finally, he got up from the chair he was sitting in, walked down the stairs of the porch, unzipped his fly, retrieved his penis and took a piss in front of forty or more people. When he was finished, he put his penis back in his trousers and apologized to everyone there, saying that all of his life he had worshiped Elizabeth Taylor and that he was so intimidated working with her that he couldn't function, so he had thought that if he did something outrageous, such as urinating in front of everyone, he could most likely do anything! He then returned to the porch and filmed the scene in one take!

SHAKESPEARE AND THE FUNNY MAN

It has been rumored that Sir Laurence Olivier and Danny Kaye had a ten-year sexual affair with each other, even though both their families and many of their friends have denied it. It seems quite

Danny Kaye

plausible that such a rumor is just that, a rumor, since both of those incredibly talented men were poles apart in their performance areas. Olivier was an international actor playing Hamlet and Othello. Kaye was a comedian and an actor on stage and in films and later in his life achieved icon status, as did Olivier. Even if those two were homosexual or bisexual, it is hard to believe or fathom what in the world would bring two such different people together. Rumors circulate about many actors' sexuality and preferences, even when there is no basis for the rumor.

Both men were married, Olivier to Vivien Leigh, and Kaye to Sylvia, whom he met while working in an off-Broadway play in 1939. Both had children. Kaye won so many awards and honors that it would take pages to list them all. He was knighted by Queen Margrethe II of Denmark in 1983 for his 1952 portrayal of Hans Christian Andersen in the film of the same name. You could have called him Sir Danny Kaye, which would definitely have been an honor for a Jewish boy from Brooklyn named David Daniel Kaminsky. He also received the French Legion of Honor for his work with UNICEF. Ronald Reagan posthumously awarded him the Presidential Medal of Freedom, America's highest civilian award. Many other awards and honors were bestowed upon him.

Laurence Olivier

Olivier was widely regarded as one of the best actors of the twentieth century. He won an Oscar for the film *Hamlet* in 1948 and was nominated thirteen times for the Academy Award, nine times as best actor, once for supporting actor, twice for best picture and once for best director. He was knighted by Queen Elizabeth II, created a "life peer" in 1970, and awarded the Order of Merit in 1981. With all of his and Kaye's achievements and awards the rumors still persist. A biography of Vivien Leigh alleges that she had a breakdown when she found out about Olivier's relationship with Kaye. After Kaye and his wife separated, he became involved with a succession of women and seriously with Eve Arden, a famous actress of that period. The rumors persisted that he was either homosexual or bisexual, even though the alleged relationship was denied by Olivier's official biographer. Joan Plowright, Olivier's last wife, often deflected such questions about him; however, in her memoirs she denies that there had been an affair between the two men. In an interview in August of 2006, long after Olivier had passed, she responded to the allegations about his mistresses and his homosexual affairs by saying, "I don't think there is any need to defend his memory. His performances, his greatness as an artist are there." She also wrote in relation to the rumors, "If a man is touched by genius, he is not an ordinary person. He doesn't lead an ordinary life. He has extremes of behavior which you understand and you just find a way not to be swept overboard by his demons. You kind of stand apart. You continue your own work and your absorption in the family. And those other things finally don't matter."

Danny Kaye's final girlfriend, Marlene Sorosky, reported that he told her, "I've never had a homosexual experience in my life. I've never had any kind of gay relationship. I've had opportunities, but I never did anything about them." Whether it makes any difference in what one believes or not, people's private lives should not be entangled in their public lives. Both those men were giants and should be revered as giants.

DINING WITH SIR LAURENCE OLIVIER

Another group of interesting tales have filtered down through decades from one person to another. What alterations they may have received in the retelling is hard to define. I have heard a couple and have retold them to my students and friends. Here are two that I have really enjoyed:

During the making of *Marathon Man,* Dustin Hoffman and Laurence Olivier were having dinner together. Sir Laurence was totally involved in his food, while Dustin was chatting with him about a number of things. At one point Hoffman asked Olivier,

"Larry, why do we do this? What makes us choose this as a profession? Why do we want to act?" All the while Olivier was totally involved with his food, never looking up at Hoffman. Finally, he raised his head, put his fork down and with Shakespearean gestures and the enunciation to match said, "Look at me! Look at me! Look at me!" Without flinching he went back to his plate.

One morning on the same film Dustin appeared unshaven, completely exhausted, disheveled and pale. Olivier looked at him and asked him what had happened to him. Hoffman replied that he had stayed up all night and hadn't washed or shaved in order to prepare for the upcoming scene, where he had to be in that state. At that point, taking a theatrical moment, Olivier said, "Well, Dustin, have you ever tried acting?"

I don't know how Dustin Hoffman works, but it certainly sounds as if he is Method oriented. I know, on the other hand, that Olivier was very anti-Method! He made that clear at every opportunity. I know that Marilyn Monroe had a tough time on the film she did with him, *The Prince and the Showgirl* (although I have to say her insecurities also created a lot of difficulties for the cast and crew). Olivier was definitely a great actor, and that greatness came from the amount of talent he was endowed with, but I seriously wonder whether he had an organic technique, a process that stimulates reality, rather than a finely developed technical approach to everything he did.

A METHOD OR NOT A METHOD, THAT IS THE QUESTION

Stories circulate around Hollywood year after year, and it is hard to tell whether they are true and accurate after traveling from person to person. People have a tendency to embellish a story until it has more facets than the original.

While doing *On Golden Pond* with her father, Henry, Jane Fonda approached him just prior to doing a scene with him and since she has a Method background, asked him if he would like to do some preparation with her before shooting the scene. Henry rose from his director's chair, looked at Jane, sternly announced, "I'm not that kind of actor!" and walked away. Mumbling under her breath, Jane said, "Yes you are, Dad; you just don't know it!"

WAS IT SELF-DEFENSE, OR WHO DID IT?

This rumor has been circulating for over five decades: Lana Turner was married eight times, which I think must be some kind of record—or if it's not, it should be! In 1958 her daughter, Cheryl Crane, admitted that she had stabbed to death Johnny Stompanato, a known criminal, to save her mother, who was being savagely beaten by him. She was acquitted of all charges, and the deed was written off as an act of protective self-defense. The persisting rumor, however, was that Lana Turner had been having a lover's quarrel with Johnny, which had escalated into violence, and she had stabbed him to death. Of course, if that reality had been admitted, Lana would indeed have been prosecuted for second-degree murder or at the very least manslaughter, not to mention it would have completely sunk her career. The Hollywood PR machine immediately took over and reasoned that if Cheryl, a young innocent girl, had been defending her mother's life, that would certainly be taken into account, and the whole thing would go away. After all, Stompanato was a notorious gangster and the world would most likely be better off without him. However, as a result of the whole affair, Lana's career did suffer. One might wonder what the hell she was doing with Johnny in the first place!

OVERHEARD IN A POSH RESTAURANT

This is another hearsay story that has been passed down from one person to another: Carol Lynley, an actress who had a career in Hollywood in the sixties, seventies and eighties and whom I was actually in a film with, was having dinner in a Beverly Hills restaurant. She was in the midst of a heated argument with the man who accompanied her. When the argument escalated to a high enough volume to be heard by many of the people dining at nearby tables, he said in a loud and angry voice, "You are a fucking bore," to which she responded, "And you are a boring fuck!"

WHAT ADVICE WOULD YOU GIVE A YOUNG ACTOR?

Young actors at the beginning of their careers want advice from actors who have been successful and whom they admire. The following stories are just a few that have been humorously circulated over the years:

A young actor approached Spencer Tracy and asked him for advice about acting.

"Don't look at the floor for your marks and don't bump into the furniture!" Tracy said. I don't know if he was sincere or just being funny.

The same question was put to James Cagney by a young hopeful. Cagney responded, "Look the other actor straight in the eyes and tell the truth!" I personally think that is good advice.

On "The Merv Griffin Show," Merv Griffin asked Al Pacino, "How did you get from the Bronx to Broadway?"

Pacino responded, "By subway!"

When Bette Davis was approached by a young actress asking for advice, she said, "Take Fountain." (Fountain Avenue is a street that runs east-west in Hollywood.)

OTHER FASCINATING PEOPLE WHO CROSSED MY PATH

When I look back on my life and a very long career, I realize how fortunate I have been to have encountered so many interesting and talented people. Riches go beyond gold and material wealth. The memories I have and the rich experiences I shared throughout my life are what life's gift really is. The final structure of my personality is related to the impact that all of these people have had on me.

MACHO ACTOR IN BALLET TIGHTS

Robert Ryan

In 1957 I took a ballet class hoping to help my body be more relaxed and fluid. The teacher, Nico Charise, looked like Zorba the Greek. His salt-and-pepper hair, which seemed to have a life of its own, stood many inches into the air, with wings emanating from the sides of his head. His nose was large and his lips generous. He spoke with an accent and dressed in ballet attire.

Standing four feet away from me was Robert Ryan in black skin-tight tights and ballet slippers. When I first recognized him, I was taken aback by what I thought in the beginning was an apparition. Robert Ryan was a movie star known for his versatility as a character actor. He played everything, from a bigoted psycho killer to western gunmen and generals in the army. He must have done a hundred films in his career, and he was always good. When I first saw him, I had to stifle a laugh. I had watched him for years on the screen, and seeing him now in the fifth position with his arms uplifted, doing ballet movements, was totally disorienting! My experience with him had been completely different.

As far as my talent for ballet, I must have looked like a hippo in a Walt Disney animated feature, stumbling around that hardwood floor trying to follow Nico's directions. Ryan, on the other hand, looked pretty good, moving with grace and using his body almost as a trained dancer would. My problem was that I couldn't separate my image of him from how I saw him as a film actor. My ballet career was short-lived, and I really believe that when I left the class Nico breathed a sigh of relief.

THE ROBERT BLAKE THAT I KNEW

Robert Blake

I met "Bobby" Blake in 1957 or '58 at the Players' Ring Theatre when I was stage-managing *Girls of Summer*. I explained earlier how almost every evening at intermission Blake and Stockwell would appear to see Driscoll. After a couple of weeks I had injected myself into the trio and was accepted as one of them. They spoke about many things, about the old days working with big stars in films such as *The Treasure of the Sierra Madre*, in which Blake appeared as a small boy. Blake talked about Humphrey Bogart and John Huston and how they worked with him. I remembered having seen Dean Stockwell in *The Boy with Green Hair* and having been impressed by his work in that film.

A couple of years after the play closed, while I was in Martin Landau's acting class, I met Sandra Knight, who was incredibly beautiful and talented. We did a number of scenes together in that class and would rehearse at her apartment in Hollywood. She was living with Blake at the time, and he would appear now and again. Since he remembered me from our backstage sessions, we would sit and talk with each other. He was always open and sensitive with me. I liked him and thought that he was enormously talented. At one of those rehearsals with Sandra, Bobby asked if he could interrupt us to watch a show he had done recently on television. We all sat and watched him. I liked what he did, but he was quite critical of his work. At the end he said it was worth watching because he learned a lot from what he saw and in the future would address what he didn't like in his performance. We liked each other so much that he and Sandra and my wife and I spent a weekend together in Lake Arrowhead. We rented a cabin and sat by the fire, avoiding the cold outside, sharing stories and drinking wine. It was a memorable weekend, and the feelings of the time stayed with me for a very long while. I lost contact with Bobby after that. Sandra left him and got involved with Jack Nicholson, who was also in our acting class. She and Jack were married not long after. I was at their wedding in a little house on Hampton Avenue in Hollywood.

What happened in Blake's life could be classified as a Hollywood tragedy. I always felt bad for him because of what he went through.

WAS SHE ADOPTED OR NOT?

We were sitting at an outdoor restaurant on the Sunset Strip. It was late afternoon and the sun had just slipped behind one of the hills above the strip. Four of us, who had been in Martin Landau's workshop the night before, had gathered there for lunch to discuss acting and possibly find scenes we could do in class. I was drinking coffee and was reluctant to order any food from that greasy spoon. The others were eating hot dogs and hamburgers. Only Judy and I had passed on the food. Judy had only taken a couple of classes, and she wasn't even sure whether she would continue in

Martin's. I told her that the class and the work had had an incredible impact on my life and my work.

Judy had short blond hair that caressed her face. The ends dipped gently into the bottom of her ears. I was instantly attracted to her and found her interesting, articulate, and very sweet. She had an uncanny resemblance to Loretta Young. Her eyes, nose, and mouth were a perfect match for Loretta's, and had she been a brunette, the resemblance would have been complete. At that point I didn't think that it was anything but a coincidence. Scores of people look like other people, and there are certainly many movie-stars' look-alikes.

That was my only encounter with Judy Lewis, since she didn't enroll in the class. A number of years went by, until what was a well-kept secret broke through the membrane of silence and it became known that Judy was the daughter of Clark Gable and Loretta Young. As the story goes, Gable and Loretta had an affair while making *Call of the Wild* on location, and Loretta got pregnant. In those days her career would have suffered a fatal blow if it had been known that she had become pregnant from a famous actor who was married. As a matter of fact, her contract had a morality clause that would have sunk her career. Her mother therefore whisked her off to Europe, where she delivered her baby girl. Returning to America, she announced that she was adopting a child, and when she married Mr. Lewis, Judy was given his name and for many years thought she had been adopted.

Gable only visited her a couple of times. The first time, when she was an infant, he discovered her sleeping in a drawer, so he promptly had a bed delivered to Loretta's house. The second time, Judy was about ten or eleven, and without knowing he was her biological father, she found him sweet and loving. That was the last time she ever saw him. Somewhere down the line I heard about the whole thing and had a vague image of her sitting at that table with me in 1959. Recently I read that she had died. She had become a psychologist and had been practicing for many years. A wave of sadness washed over me as I read her obituary.

HEY, WHAT'S HAPPENING, MAN?

Bruce Dern

It was a hot August night in 1960 or thereabout. I was taking a brisk walk, going east on Sunset Boulevard. As I walked by the Normandy Village, which at the time was a group of apartments on Sunset east of La Cienega, I passed a shirtless guy, who was dressed in clam-digger pants and looked much like a street person. As I went by him, he called out to me, "Hey, what's happening, man?" I kept walking, thinking he was a panhandler about to ask me for some spare change, but then I heard him shout after me, "Hey, you're an actor?" That stopped me cold. I turned around as he walked towards me, and when he was about two feet away, he said, "Yeah, I'm an actor. Just got here yesterday from New York. You look like an actor, so I asked you what is happening here!"

His name was Bruce Dern, and that was our first meeting. We chatted for a while and then I went on with my walk. Over a period of time we would run into each other and talk. Just about that time, in the early sixties, I asked Bruce to direct a play that I was putting together, *End as a Man.* I wanted Jack Nicholson to play the lead character, Jocko De Paris, but he got a part in a Roger Corman motorcycle film, so I took over the role of Jocko. We rehearsed in my apartment on Detroit Street, since none of us had any money to pay for a rehearsal space.

Bruce was a very good but demanding director, and I loved what he was doing; but some of the other members of the cast were intimidated by his demand for truth and reality, and they threatened to drop out of the play unless we got another director. I went to Bruce with the problem, and he opted to withdraw from directing the play. I was very sad, because to this day I really believe it would have been a better play if he had stayed. I would run into him at the counter at Schwab's Pharmacy, and we would talk about the business. Bruce has had a wonderful career and has done some really impressive work. I believe he has left a huge footprint as an actor in our world.

HOW ACTORS SPEND THEIR MONEY

Vic Tayback

I knew him from around town in the old days, the sixties and seventies. Hollywood was a small town. Far fewer actors were competing for roles, and many of us crossed paths on a weekly basis. Actors are a lonely breed and seek their own kind to hang out with. There was Cyrano's on the Sunset Strip, Googie's also on the strip, Schwab's drugstore and restaurant, and a half-dozen other places to find each other. We sat, drank coffee, talked about the business and bragged about our latest audition—mostly bullshit, but it was a way of feeling important when we weren't, saying things such as, "I nailed it! Blew them away. You should have seen the look on their faces when I finished the reading!" It was a way of dealing with the sense of being alone and unemployed. Most of us lived off our unemployment payments, at least until they ran out, and then we sought part-time work that would not interfere with a possible audition. Of course, no one admitted to working at anything other than acting.

Occasionally I would run into Vic Tayback, and we would either stand in front of Schwab's for a few minutes or sit drinking coffee together. Vic was stocky, solidly built and very much resembled someone you might run into on a New York street. He had a simian quality, but was actually more like a teddy bear than a gorilla. In a TV show or on stage, his eyes were alive with a kind of tension, which calmed down in later years.

Vic came to see *End as a Man,* and was so impressed with my work that he invited me to become a member of The Angels Company, a very popular group known for doing very good work. I was flattered and took him up on the invitation. Unfortunately, I never auditioned for any of their plays and only stayed there for less than a year. Vic and I were also at the Actors Studio together.

Vic landed a role in the movie *Alice Doesn't Live Here Anymore*, in which he played the cook in the restaurant. When the film was later made into a TV series called "Alice," Vic played the same character for over two hundred episodes. He was very good in it. The role fit him like a glove, and he was very funny, besides being a good actor. The series ran from 1976 to 1985. If you know anything about residuals and the like, you'll know that after five years all the running roles on a series become millionaires. As do a large number of actors who make it and get rich, instead of buying a yacht or a Ferrari, Vic bought race horses and, as far as I know, actually raced them.

Racing is called the sport of kings, and it takes a king's income to support it. I really don't know how successful Vic was in that venture, since we lost contact in later years. Whenever I think about him, it is always with affection. He is one of the many actors I grew up with in Hollywood, so many of whom are gone. Vic died in 1990 at the age of 60.

A MAN OF MANY CONTRADICTIONS

I met Curt Conway in the early sixties. He was referred to me by my teacher Martin Landau. Curt was in his fifties at the time and sported a full head of white hair that he combed straight back. He had a voice that sounded like a tractor grinding through a field of gravel. He was direct and blunt and had a personality that wavered between soft affability and the threat of aggressive hostility. He had been a fairly successful Broadway actor but had been blacklisted by HUAC, and because he was unable to get work as an actor, he had turned to teaching and had taught for a number of years in New York. Marty was one of his students. When Curt decided to come to Hollywood, he contacted Marty and asked him for the name of one of his students who was prominent and popular in his class. Marty told Curt about me. Curt had a couple of reasons for contacting me: one was that I might be instrumental in helping him build a class in Los Angeles, and the other, that he hated teaching beginners and wanted someone to do that.

After visiting my small class, he wrote me a note telling me that he thought I was "a born teacher" and asking if I would work for him. I jumped at the opportunity, since I had only been teaching for a very short time and was struggling to build a large enough class to make enough money to pay the rent on the place I was using. I did start teaching as an associate of Curt, and the class built rather quickly.

A lot happened in that relationship, which I wrote about in detail in my book *The Diary of a Professional Experiencer.* Because he was blacklisted and couldn't act anymore, Curt had started drinking and become a confirmed alcoholic, which probably accounted for his gravel voice. When he got drunk, he was quite mean and abusive and would say very ugly things to people. He was that way with me only once, and once was quite enough! His mother, whom we hired to collect the money from the students, was a quiet, unassuming woman in her eighties, who was totally committed to Curt. His brother, Bert Conway, also an actor, seemed to be an "also ran" and certainly not the favorite son.

While Curt had a less-than-attractive personality, he was also a man of principle, who had a large vein of nobility running through him. He refused to name names for HUAC at great cost to himself. While he was married to Kim Stanley, she had an affair that produced a boy child. Curt claimed paternity to avoid a scandal that might have ruined her career. Her affair was with the brother of Montgomery Clift, Brooks Clift, who incidentally became a dear friend of mine many years later. Curt was somewhat of an enigma. On the one hand he could be a raging alcoholic, difficult to tolerate, and on the other, a man who could sacrifice himself for the benefit of others.

SHIRLEY, IT'S SHELLEY

A whole book could be written about Shelley Winters, whose real name was Shirley Schrift. Numerous stories about her are floating around, and if you spoke to any number of actors, I'm confident that each one would have at least one interesting story about her.

I'll start with my own experiences with her. I knew Shelley for many years, at first through her sister Blanche, who was married to George Boroff. George's major claim to fame was that he owned the Circle Theater, a theater in the round where many actors got their start by being seen in plays. George was a strange bird. Curt Conway and I leased the theater for our classes, and quite often George would appear, his favorite activity being to ensnare you to walk around the block with him. On the journey he would fill you in on all the great productions done at his theater and on his participation in many of them. Of course, he would drop a famous name whenever possible. If I saw him before he saw me, I ran for cover and stayed hidden until he disappeared.

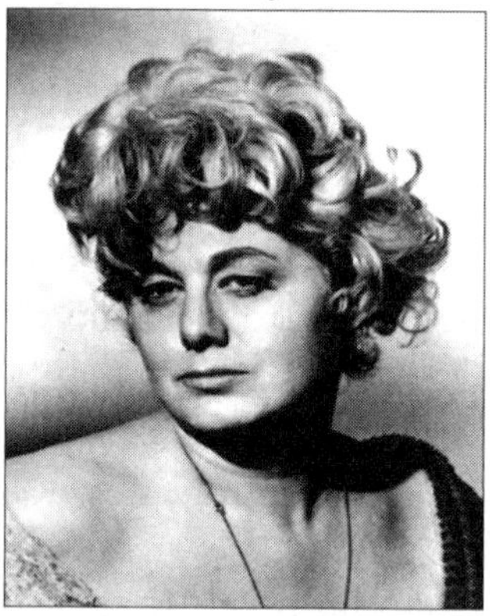
Shelley Winters

Shelley called me once at the theater and asked me if her boyfriend Richard could come and take a class from me. She told me that she was on the audition committee at the Actors Studio, and that everyone who auditioned there and claimed to have trained with me did the best work. I was flattered and told her that Richard was welcome. But he never showed up. That was one of my early encounters with Shelley.

Over a period of years we would sit at a table in a restaurant with a group of other actors. She could never remember my name. Once, when she was introducing Ernie Martin as the moderator at the Actors Studio, she introduced him as Eric Morris!

She related an interesting story to me one afternoon between her salad and entrée: While shooting *A Place in the Sun* with Montgomery Clift, she got the flu. She was in bed when Monty called her and informed her that if she didn't get down to the set immediately, the director was going to cut the scene. It was a very important scene, so she jumped out of bed and hurried to the set!

A close friend of hers recently told me this story: Her husband at the time, Vittorio Gassman, was doing Hamlet in Italy and invited her to a performance. When she joined him backstage after the show, he asked her what she thought of his performance. She told him in no uncertain terms that he stunk, so he socked her in the mouth. Shortly after that, they got divorced.

Another fascinating event happened when she was on Johnny Carson's show sharing the stage with Oliver Reed. Reed made the comment that women belonged in the kitchen and not on the stage. Shelley got up, disappeared for a few minutes, and returned with a full glass of what looked like wine, which she poured all over Reed's head. He sat there quite composed, licking the dripping liquid as it ran down his face. That was on live television.

THE FACTORY WASN'T REALLY A FACTORY

In the late sixties and early seventies a number of upscale discos could be found in Los Angeles and Beverly Hills and scattered around Southern California. The Daisy in Beverly Hills and the Factory in West Hollywood both catered to movie stars and other famous people, mostly in the motion-picture industry. At that time I was married to my first wife, and we were living in the Valley. I was teaching in Hollywood and had heard stories about those discos and how fabulous they were. I later found out that they used live bands there instead of records.

One of my students, whose name was Mark, was the son of a famous jeweler in Beverly Hills, whose clientele ranged from Elizabeth Taylor to almost every other actor in Hollywood. Mark invited me to go with him as his guest to the Factory, which was housed in a building that had once been an actual factory. What they had manufactured there, however, is still a mystery to this day. Those upscale discos were membership only, and it was difficult to become a member; but now, forty years later, I don't remember why or what the criteria were.

My first experience there was awesome. You entered on the ground floor and took an elevator up to the main space, which consisted of a large and beautifully decorated dining area with lavish furniture, drapery, tables and chairs, a bandstand and a dance floor. Other sections were arranged for quiet conversation, and the place also included a bar, as well as several pool tables. The entire atmosphere was made for comfort and enjoyment. I later learned that it was the creation of Ron Buck, whose silent partner was Paul Newman. Buck was a businessman involved in a number of real-estate ventures, one of which was the 9000 building on Sunset Boulevard, a very tall building with twenty or thirty floors. At the top, identifying the structure, is a very large 9000 that can be seen from a distance. Mark invited me to join him at the Factory a few times, and I became obsessed with wanting to become a member. I'm not sure why I was so adamant about joining, but it became incredibly important to me. At that point in my career I was acting and teaching, but I had not yet established a name or the reputation that was to come in the following decades, so maybe I felt that I needed to be surrounded by the success I was striving for. At any rate, I finally did become a member, but I don't recall how that came about. I went there as often as I could, mostly on weekends, when there were a lot of people there. I took my wife and my cousin Lee and ran up a restaurant bill that was hard to deal with at times. My cousin was impressed with all the celebrities, and in a way I felt a certain pride about being able to take him and his wife there. In a short time I felt that I was part of the place. I loved being able to drop in whenever I could. It seemed as though I had a "gentlemen's club," like those you see in British movies. Since I have never drunk alcohol, I always had a Coke and sometimes sat alone on one of the huge sofas that adorned the place. At those times I felt rich and pampered, but I was always ready to meet, talk to, or play pool with whoever would show up.

Sammy Davis Jr.

One evening I was invited to shoot pool with Sammy Davis, Jr., who played better with one eye than I did with two. He was really good. I was more interested in him than in the game. He spoke about some really personal things, about his life and his career and what he thought was important in life. He was curious about me, and when I told him that I taught acting, he was really interested in hearing about what I did, since being a good actor was extremely important to him. He admitted that most people related to him as an entertainer and not specifically as an actor. I told him that I had been an actor long before I had started teaching, but because I had some viability as a teacher, I too was typed that way. After a couple of games of eight ball in which I was embarrassingly defeated, we sat and had drinks and talked for a couple of hours. He was very down-to-earth and didn't seem at all self-impressed. After that evening and my embarrassing defeat at the pool table, I ran into Sammy several more times. He was always very friendly, and he impressed me with his memory of the things I had shared with him.

One evening I played pool with Tommy Smothers of the Smothers Brothers team, and that time I was competitive, since he was nowhere as good as Sammy. Robert Duvall showed up on a weekday evening when I happened to drop by. I knew him in passing but had never had any conversation with him before that evening. We played pool and talked. I was very impressed with his acting, and I thought not only that he was a very fine actor, but that he had a unique quality in his work that was very compelling.

During one of our games he told me a very interesting story about an experience he had doing a film with Edward Dmytryk, a director with a very forceful reputation, who "took no prisoners." Dmytryk had done many important films in his career, such as *The Young Lions, The Caine Mutiny, Anzio,* and fifty-three other films. Duvall was working with him and had a very over-the-top emotional scene. As an actor I knew exactly what he was talking about. The emotional obligation of a scene like the one he described comes from the deepest places in an actor's reservoir. Duvall told Dmytryk that he could give him exactly what he wanted but could only get to that depth once, so he asked him to make sure that all of the technical elements were ready and that they would record what he did the first time. Duvall did his preparations, and when Dmytryk called action, Duvall delivered the most impacting work, and it was terrific, but as luck would have it, the camera or the sound or something went wrong, and they had to do it over again. Duvall told me that he was very disappointed, and that when he did it the second time it wasn't what he had been able to pull up the first time. However, it was tremendously effective, and everyone on the set was extremely moved by his work. As the decades have passed, Robert Duvall's career has maintained itself, and his work is constantly impressive.

The week of the Academy Awards, as I was sitting at a table at the Factory with my wife and a couple of other friends, Rod Steiger entered the room, and all heads turned to see him. He had just won the best-actor award for that year, and there was an outburst of applause as he made his way to a table. He waved in appreciation for the ovation and sat down. Within ten minutes a dozen bottles of wine were brought to his table, covering its entire surface.

An interesting addendum to this story is that, not too long after, Ron Buck called me and asked me to meet him at a restaurant on La Brea Avenue called Hampton's, which, as I learned later, was also owned by him and Paul Newman. When I received the call, I thought it had something to do with my membership at the Factory, but as I later learned, Buck didn't even know I belonged to the club. He had heard about me as an acting teacher, and I had been highly recommended to him. As we sat and ate, he told me that his eighteen-year-old son wanted to pursue acting, and he asked me if I would meet his son and admit him into my class. I of course agreed, and his son started attending one of my classes, but it was a short-lived involvement. The last time I spoke to Ron Buck was when he called me to let me know that the club was closing. Just shortly after that the disco craze powered down to a whisper.

"LIVE FAST, DIE YOUNG AND HAVE A GOOD-LOOKING CORPSE"

Those lines were spoken by John Derek in his first movie *Knock on Any Door*. The incredibly good-looking Derek played a hoodlum, a gangster who ends up being sentenced to death for murdering someone. The film, which also starred Humphrey Bogart, made John Derek a movie star. After that, he did a rash of movies, playing all kinds of characters.

He was into beautiful women, and he started to photograph them. One of them was Ursula Andress, with whom he was also romantically involved. Later in his life he married Bo Derek, who starred in the movie *10* and was really a number ten! I believe that his love for beautiful women was paramount in his life and all of his pursuits. I met him only once at the Daisy, a members-only discotheque in Beverly Hills. He had somehow met a young woman I was involved with at the time—probably one of the ten most beautiful women in the world—and he had asked her to meet him for a drink at the Daisy. Since she knew his reputation and was in love with me besides, she had asked me to accompany her. He was surprised and a little miffed to see me walk through the door with her. He smiled at her and disregarded my presence, until she introduced me as her boyfriend, which upset him even more. She told him that I was also her acting teacher and that she liked his work. He looked at me and then at her, a little at a loss as to where to go from there. He asked her if he could come to my class and watch her work.

She looked at me, then at him, and said, "You have to ask Eric if you could visit the class."

This really pissed him off. "Do I have to get permission from the pope to come to your class?" he asked.

That question was directed at me, so I smiled and told him that he was welcome to come to my class any time he wanted to. My response defused the situation, and he invited us to sit and have a drink with him. In the next forty minutes he spoke only to her and never once even looked at me.

THE ACTOR, THE PREACHER, THE TEACHER

Otis Young

A black actor with striking features, in his younger years he was angry and ready to get into any kind of argument with you if he thought you were being offensive, even if you had really only made an innocent comment about the weather. His name was Otis Young, and I had seen his work even before we met. He was talented and compelling to watch. Even though we had passed each other around town, as actors did in those days, my first experience with him was on the film *Survival* in 1976. I had been hired by the director, Michael Campus, to help cast the film and be its associate producer. It was Michael's directorial debut, and he wanted someone to back him up with the actors. The film told an interesting story, which took place in one room of a big house, with all the actors sitting around a large table. It had quite a good cast: Anne Francis, Barry Sullivan, Sheree North, Chuck McCann, Susanne Benton, my friend Hampton Fancher, and of course Otis.

After they started shooting, I watched the filming of each scene, trying to be as unobtrusive as possible. One day, while I was observing, Otis turned to me and in front of the whole cast and crew said, "Those who can, do and those who can't, teach." There was an uncomfortable silence on the set. Deeply hurt and embarrassed, I left the room. I continued on the film, but Otis and I walked a wide track around each other from then on. I didn't see Otis after that, but I knew that he was a busy working actor in films and television. His credits dated back to 1963. He had done some major films in his career, including *The Last Detail* with Jack Nicholson.

Many years passed. In the early nineties I received a call from Otis, who was then teaching speech and theater at a community college in Rochester, New York, where he was also directing some of the students in plays. He told me that the acting teachers at the college knew nothing about the subject, and he asked if I would please send him some of my books, so that those teachers might learn something about what they were teaching. We had an interesting conversation. I asked him what he had been doing since he had left Hollywood, and he told me that he had become the senior pastor at the Elm Foursquare Church in Rochester and that he had preached there from 1986 to 1988 when he left and started teaching at the college. He didn't tell me why he had left preaching to become a teacher; I had to use my imagination on that issue. At any rate, I sent him several of my books, along with a little note saying, "Well, Otis, those who can't preach teach." A few days later I received a response with just one word, "Touché." Otis's last film was in 2001 after a long layoff. It was called *After Image.*

He died of a stroke in 2001 at the age of sixty-nine. When I heard about his death, I was very sad.

THE SCHWARZENEGGER CHRONICLES

Sometime around 1976 I received a call from Bob Rafelson who was directing a film called *Stay Hungry,* starring Jeff Bridges and Sally Field. A large part of the story in the film centered on the Mr. Olympia competition, and Rafelson wanted to use Arnold Schwarzenegger, who had already won that competition more than once. Bob told me that Arnold was perfect for the role but that he had very little acting experience. If Arnold worked with an acting coach, however, Rafelson felt he would be able to get the performance he wanted. Since Jack Nicholson had worked with Rafelson on *Five Easy Pieces,* Bob had asked Jack to recommend a coach, and Jack had told him to contact me. I asked Rafelson how much time I had to work with Arnold, and he told me that they would start filming nine weeks later. I responded that it was a very short time for anyone to digest and be able to apply my work and that I might confuse Arnold instead of helping him. Bob retorted that I had come highly recommended by Jack and that he respected my honesty; but would I at least meet with Arnold?

Arnold Schwarzenegger

I hadn't the vaguest idea who Arnold was at that point, since I had never followed the bodybuilding community. Rafelson described him to me, and I met him at my studio soon after that. We hit it off from the very first meeting. We liked each other immediately, and I started to work with him three or four times a week. Because of the way I work, we did not address the script for the first six weeks. Instead, I talked to Arnold about his whole life, from childhood to that time. I needed to understand him and the things that had influenced his evolution as a person. I was gathering information that could later be translated as "choices" for the character and the obligations of the scenes in the film. Arnold was very open and related many things about his life to me. He loved his mother and had less affection for his father, a policeman in the village they lived in, who had been very strict with his son while he was growing up. Arnold told me how bodybuilding had become a much-needed perk in his life and how he worked out feverishly every day. He would beg his mother to buy meat so that he could add as much protein as was necessary to support his muscle growth. He was so adamant about his workout that one Sunday, when the gym was closed, he climbed on the roof and broke into the place through the skylight!

We also talked about his friends, school, and the anti-Semitism he was exposed to during his childhood. The books the students were issued had pictures of ugly, disease-riddled Jews with distorted features and bodies. A side note here and an issue that I must address at this point: I have known Arnold for over thirty-six years. He does not have an anti-Semitic bone in his body, and he spends time and money supporting the Jewish congregation of Rabbi Hier, the founder of the Simon Wiesenthal Center. He also told me a funny story about his military service in Austria, which was mandatory. He drove a tank into a brick wall and bent the cannon, and that was the end of his service!

I found Arnold to be incredibly intelligent, with a business acumen that was so impressive I started to ask him questions about my financial well-being. When we finally got to the script, I broke it down scene for scene and worked with the choices I had gleaned from our six weeks of exploration of his life. He did that film and won a Golden Globe Award for the most promising newcomer of that year. I was extremely proud of him.

After the film was finished, he came to study with me in my group classes. At that time I was teaching in a studio space that was configured in the shape of a horseshoe, so the actors would work in the stage area, surrounded on three sides by all the other students. Arnold came every week and did everything I asked him to do and, as he does with everything he works on, he gave it his total commitment. One evening he came into the class obviously disturbed and angry. He could hardly sit still. I saw what was going on and asked him to work first. He stood up, looked at me, and waited for me to say something to him.

"Arnold," I said, "what's going on? You look very upset." He had just come from an interview with an agent whom he was trying to get to represent him.

"I am pissed off!" he responded. "They don't like my name, they don't like my accent, and they don't like my body. So fuck them, I am going to be a superstar!"

He was breathing fire, and when he finished, everyone in class stood up and applauded him.

Over a period of time I had given him a variety of exercises and material, and it was quite obvious how really talented he was. That time after *Stay Hungry* was a difficult time for him, but when he finally got several action-adventure roles, his career took off.

One evening sticks out in my memory: Arnold had left the class after eight or nine months and was pursuing work. He visited my class, and we went out for Mexican food. A whole group of us were sitting at the table. Arnold's charisma lights up whatever environment he visits. He told me that he really respected me and loved my work but that he wanted to do action-adventure films, because he was very physical and felt that he would do well in that area. I told him that I understood totally and wished him well.

Many years have passed since that evening. Arnold has become an icon and somewhat of a legend. Some years ago we met at Café Roma in Beverly Hills, one of Arnold's favorite restaurants. We sat and spoke about many things. When three well-dressed men appeared, Arnold looked at me and said, "Here come the suits!" His friend Ralf Moeller and a couple of others were at the table, and Arnold asked me if I would teach Ralf how to tell a joke and lighten up. I told Arnold that I thought his next endeavor was politics and that he would run for governor of California. He shook his head, smiled and said, "No, Eric, I am not interested in politics." That was just about two years before he announced on a late-night talk show that he would run for that office. At this point one might think I am psychic or have a crystal ball, but neither of those is true. I just knew Arnold and that once he had reached the pinnacle of success in one area, such as bodybuilding or the movies, he would find another mountain to climb. We spoke about acting, and he told me that as he would be getting older he would like to do more serious acting, roles with great depth and emotion. I told him that I was sure he could do that quite successfully.

As time passed, he ran for the governorship and was elected twice. He called me from the governor's office one day and asked if I could teach his daughter, and of course I said yes. Unfortunately, our schedules never worked out, because she was in school and could only work weekends and I did not have any classes on the weekends. I told Arnold that I was finishing a book called *The Diary of a Professional Experiencer,* and he said that he would like to write the foreword, to which I responded, "Aren't you too busy as the governor of California to take the time to write a foreword?" To which he said, "No, I want to do it!"—which he did, and I am eternally grateful. Arnold is very special, and if you really get to know him, you will find he has a huge heart and is very generous.

"EYEWITNESS TO THE PAST"

"Eyewitness to the Past" was a television series that I was hired to host, probably sometime in the early eighties. It was something like Steve Allen's show "Meeting of the Minds," where a host moderator interviewed famous people from history. I received a call from Kayla Garren, who had been a student of mine in the seventies. Kayla is a woman for all seasons. She has been an actor, an executive for a large trade paper, and a businesswoman in a variety of interesting endeavors. When she was attending my class, she did a scene with Arnold Schwarzenegger from *Sweet Bird of Youth,* in which she was excellent, as was Arnold. At the time of the call she was in partnership with Fred Thorne, running a production company. Together they were juggling several projects for television. One of them was a series based on interviewing exciting people from the past. Since Kayla knew that I was not only her teacher but also an actor that she respected, they asked me if I would be interested in being the host moderator for the series, which was to be syndicated. They had planned to do thirty-nine half-hour segments.

The show was being financed by the Mormons, but in great contradiction it was to be supervised by a Catholic priest, Father Banahan, a short and stocky guy with the map of Ireland on his forehead, who was as Irish as Paddy's pig and even had a slight Irish intonation to his speech. He was incredibly likeable and had a great sense of humor. His mistress appeared almost daily on the set and followed him around as unobtrusively as possible. She was a small, birdlike lady with curly, graying blond hair, and her head seemed to lean forward, which made her appear even more birdlike. It is common knowledge that Catholic priests are supposed to be celibate, but that was only one of the strange things about Father Banahan. The story was that he had been kicked out of Chicago by the bishop and assigned to be the PR representative for the Catholic Church, which I guess was a good way for the leadership to get rid of him, at least so that he wasn't so visible.

The way the show was structured was that each person being interviewed received a lot of information about the character he or she was doing, a complete background of that famous person's actions and impact on the world. I was given the same information on each character, and I was to ask questions related to all the details that had been provided to both the actor and me. The actual interview and the relationship between the actor and me were improvisational. There were no written lines—which made the interviews seem much more impulsive and real. One of the important perks was that I was able to use many of my students as characters on the show, and even my brother Ed Morris, who was really quite good both as Lenin and as Junípero Serra, the priest who had walked all across California and founded many missions, something he had done with a handicapped leg, which made it not only difficult but very painful. Father Banahan played John, the English king during the time of the signing of the Magna Carta.

The show was quite exciting, since I found ways to challenge and intimidate some of the characters I was interviewing. I interviewed Mary Todd Lincoln, Mussolini, Thomas Jefferson, George Washington, and a host of others. I really got into it, challenging Hitler, for example, to justify his actions. Each character was interviewed for the entire half hour. Only a couple of times did we split the time between two interviews. All of the actors wore period costumes that were appropriate for the characters they were playing, and we also had a complete makeup crew. I had hoped that the show would be syndicated in a lot of markets. I have never seen it on the air, so I am not sure where it aired. It was a great experience, however.

LUNCH AT THE SOURCE WITH A SENSITIVE AND BEAUTIFUL ACTRESS

It was a glorious day and the weather was perfect. The sun shone directly overhead and cast shadows through the fronds of the palm trees surrounding the restaurant. The shadows covered the outdoor patio like a protective umbrella, shielding all of the patrons from the hot sun. We were at the Source restaurant on the Sunset Strip, which specialized in healthy food. Sitting across from me was Susan Strasberg, whom I had met at the Actors Studio. The daughter of Lee and Paula Strasberg, she fortunately resembled Paula instead of Lee. She had written a play about Lee and Paula and Marilyn Monroe. Sally Kirkland, an actress I had known for decades, played Marilyn, and Barbara Bain was Tallulah Bankhead. I thought it was a very interesting play with a lot of talent in it.

Susan Strasberg

I was meeting Susan because she had heard that I owned a house in Lake Arrowhead and she wanted to use it to continue writing. Susan was beautiful and had an incredible résumé of work. She had made her Broadway debut in *The Diary of Anne Frank,* playing the title role, and had appeared in many films—including *Picnic* with Kim Novak and William Holden—and in dozens of television shows; but she frequently returned to the Broadway stage. At that time she was in her forties and was as beautiful as she must have been in her twenties. Her dark hair lay across her shoulders, and her eyes sparkled with a zest for life. Her skin was white with a translucent quality. I felt very excited about our meeting. Even though I knew why we were there, it was still exhilarating to be with her.

We spoke about many things: acting, teaching, her father and mother, and her very close relationship to Marilyn Monroe. I had always been very into Lee's work. Of all the master teachers, I thought he contributed the most to the actors' training. Susan told me many stories about her life and her relationships, including her marriage to Chris Jones. She also told me the following story: For a long time she had searched unsuccessfully for a certain document, a paper or possibly a letter—I don't remember exactly what it was. With tears in her eyes she said, "My father came to me in a dream and told me where to find it, and it was exactly where he had said it would be, in the most unlikely place I would have explored."

She also talked about Marilyn with great affection. She considered her part of the family. Marilyn would not do a movie unless Paula was on the set. Susan told me that she and Marilyn were like sisters. "One day we were walking down Fifth Avenue in New York," she recounted, "and nobody recognized Marilyn, even though she was at the height of her fame at the time. So I called her attention to that fact. She looked at me and explained, 'That's because I'm not being Marilyn.' She immediately took on her Marilyn persona, and everyone immediately recognized her, stopped us, and made a big fuss."

The tears ran down Susan's face, finding their way into her lips. I wanted to hug her and comfort her, but it didn't seem appropriate, so I reached across the table and squeezed her hand. She smiled and seemed grateful. She never did go up to my house in the mountains to write, even though I had told her that she could. Shortly after that, it was announced that she had died of breast cancer.

THANKSGIVING DINNER WITH SIR ANTHONY HOPKINS

Anthony Hopkins

For many years I had been very impressed with the work that Anthony Hopkins was doing. I had seen almost all of his films and hoped to meet him someday. I had even toyed with the idea of contacting his agent to ask if Hopkins would speak to my students.

Several years went by, but I never contacted him. I am not sure why, since I had been so impressed with his acting. I have never been star struck. Having been in the business for many years and also having had the pleasure of working with so many celebrities, I learned that they were people just like me, who had their own issues and problems. The more secure they were the more real and down-to-earth.

About two years ago, in 2011, I received a call from Stella Hopkins, Anthony's wife. Stella had been a student of mine in the past, but except for running into her at the airport a few years ago, I hadn't seen her for fifteen or more years. She said that "Tony" would like to meet me and possibly work with me and my students. She had told him what a wonderful teacher I was and how much she had gotten from me. Well, to say it was a mind-blowing telephone call would be putting it mildly! I was so impacted by the possibility of actually meeting Sir Anthony that I was incoherent on the phone. I think Stella said that she and her assistant would like to come by and watch my class, and she asked if I would like Tony to come too or would prefer to wait until we met first. I agreed that the second choice would be the way to do it. She kept referring to Sir Anthony as Tony and I felt that it was something like calling Queen Elizabeth "Liz." Over the years I had heard a variety of things about him, one of which was that he was a member of the Actors Studio and was a Method actor. Of course that made sense to me, since that was my orientation and justified my incredible respect for his work.

Shortly after our telephone conversation, Stella and her assistant, Jennifer, showed up to one of my evening classes. Stella told me that they could only stay for a short time, since it was such a long drive back to where she lived. They sat in the first row and watched as I conducted several instrumental exercises and one monologue. With a huge smile and a handshake, they excused themselves, telling me how impressed they were with the work I was doing and that another reason for Stella's original call was that Jennifer had expressed a desire to pursue acting and also wanted to see my work.

About a week later I received a call from Stella inviting me to the Hopkins' home in Malibu for Sunday dinner. She and Tony liked to eat dinner early, around five o'clock. She told me that they would send a car to pick us up and take us there. I felt like a kid invited to go see his first circus. I was so excited by the possibility of meeting Sir Anthony and visiting him at his home! My wife, Susana, saw how much it meant to me. We went to a liquor store and bought two bottles of the most expensive and best French wines to take with us. I was not aware at the time that Sir Anthony did not drink and had been going to AA for many years. Saturday, the day before the big event, Susana picked out the clothes that I was going to wear.

Sunday morning arrived after a sleepless night, and like a child on Christmas morning, I couldn't make the time pass fast enough. Around eleven o'clock Stella called and told me that they had to cancel because they had been working to get all of their books put away and the house was overflowing with books and manuscripts, which were all over the place. She apologized and told me that she would be in touch shortly. I was overwhelmed with disappointment and tried to hide it from Susana, very unsuccessfully. My feeling was that they had had second thoughts about our getting together. I was sure that I would never hear from them again and felt totally rejected.

A week or so later, however, I received an e-mail from Stella asking if we could have Thanksgiving dinner with her and Tony. I immediately e-mailed back that we would be delighted. Susana had already bought all the food for Thanksgiving dinner for the two of us and was not as excited about giving up her plans in order to go meet with the Hopkins. She knew, however, how important it was for me, so she agreed. After several e-mails back and forth, we arranged to meet them at the Bel Air Hotel at four o'clock on Thanksgiving Day. We got to Beverly Hills early, and I drove around for some time before pulling into the hotel parking lot. The Bel Air Hotel, an exclusive place that many famous actors frequent, had just recently finished a complete renovation. We were greeted in the lobby by Jennifer, who asked us to sit down by the fireplace and said she would come get us shortly. I was very excited and nervous at the same time. My heart rate had increased exponentially, and my mouth was dry. In just a few minutes Jennifer reappeared and led us down a hall to the suite they were in. She knocked on the door gently, and Sir Anthony opened it and greeted us both with a generous hug. He was dressed casually, and his gray hair was combed back neatly. His smile was genuine and warm. I had expected a nice handshake, not a body hug; it threw me for a minute or so. There I was in the same room with the last of the great ones, and he had hugged me! Wow!

We were ushered into a suite of rooms with a large living room, where we sat. Stella appeared from the other room and greeted us. Anthony was wearing the most colorful and outrageous shoes, which had been bought especially for the occasion, and we talked about them briefly. Several platters of finger sandwiches and dried fruit had been arranged on a very ornate table in front of us. I was too nervous to eat anything, so I did my best to look calm, natural and relaxed. Susana seemed much more comfortable than I. If she was tense at all, it was because of concern for me. I told Stella that she looked great and had not changed much from when I had first met her. She told Tony that I was the best acting teacher in the world with no runners up. I was embarrassed but flattered at the same time.

Tony told us that we were in the Grace Kelly suite, which she had used while filming in Hollywood. We talked a little about my classes and the books I had written. I told him that I really liked *The World's Fastest Indian,* a film he had done about a man from New Zealand who had souped up an Indian motorcycle and wanted to enter it at the salt flats in America to claim the speed title for it. I was particularly impressed with the accent Tony had achieved and the character of that man. He told me that it had become a cult film and was placed in a special category. Stella spoke about when she was in my class and remembered many of the things I had said to her. Tony said that he had just become a vegetarian, and I told him that I had been one for about thirty years. He said that without meat he had lost several pounds in a very short time.

During our conversation a friend of theirs knocked on the door and was greeted by Jennifer and invited into the room. A doctor originally from Colombia and a dear friend of Tony and Stella, she was effervescent and filled with energy. Her accent complemented her expression. We all sat and talked for about half an hour, at which time a well-dressed woman appeared at the door and invited us to dinner. We followed her down a long hallway bracketed by large vases containing all sorts of flowers and foliage. In the dining room we were led to a table right in front of a large fireplace. I am sure that it must be one of the VIP tables. There were six of us: Tony, Stella, Jennifer, the Colombian friend, Susana, and I. Susana sat across from Stella and next to me on my left. I was sitting next to Tony. As soon as we settled into our chairs, I told him that he was the last of the great ones, meaning actors such as Laurence Olivier, Peter O'Toole, Ralph Richardson, Ben Kingsley, Richard Burton, and many of the other legendary British actors. I added that I would love to work with him, and he responded that he would love to work with me also. For the next two hours he and I were rapt in conversation. The ladies were involved with each other and seemed to be having a good time. Three of them spoke Spanish, so their conversations moved back and forth between Spanish and English. Every once in a while Susana would run her hand across my back with reassuring affection.

I was getting more comfortable, calling Hopkins Tony instead of Sir Anthony, but it was an adjustment I had to make. He told me about his early life in Wales, growing up as a young boy during the Second World War. The American soldiers would visit with gifts of food and chocolates, but Tony was more interested about their stories of America. From early on he was enthralled with the United States, particularly California, and even as he grew older his ambition was to come and live here. He talked about his ailing mother and said that his concern with her comfort had prompted him to bring her over to California. He told me about his first movie, *The Lion in Winter* with Katharine Hepburn and Peter O'Toole. The first day on the set Hepburn had approached him and said, "Don't act!" He spoke a little about her and how direct and forceful she was in everything she did. We were really communicating, and I felt that we really liked each other, which helped to relax me so I could be who I am. I asked him about his role in Woody Allen's film *You Will Meet a Tall Dark Stranger,* and he told me that Woody had sent him the script after offering him the role, which was a surprise to me, since I had heard numerous times that Woody Allen never gave his actors a complete script. Tony said that the first scene he had shot in the film was with the actress playing his ex-wife and that it was well into the film. Because he is such a great actor, however, no one would think that was his first scene, since he embodies the entire history of the relationship at that table in that restaurant. He launched into doing Woody Allen talking to him while shooting the film, and he did Woody better than Woody himself! I discovered that one of the facets of his talent is to be able to mimic and get a real sense of other people. He is able to take on their physical characteristics as well as their voice and mannerisms.

During all of that intense conversation, dinner was served. I don't know what the traditional turkey dinner was like, but the vegetarian food was awful! It consisted of little round things that seemed to have been compressed into a hard hockey-puck configuration of what appeared to be unidentifiable vegetables. The pastries were the best part of the meal. I could see that Stella was disappointed in the fare but said nothing. Every once in a while I included the ladies in the conversation. Stella told us that Tony was quite an artist and that she had discovered his talent for art because he would draw pictures on the blank pages of his film script while shooting a film. She encouraged him to start painting and ultimately opened a gallery in Hawaii that was very successful in selling his work. I also learned that he was a very accomplished musician at the piano. He had recorded a symphonic piece with a well-established classical orchestra, playing the piano with them. There seemed to be no end to that man's talent. I felt that I was in the presence of greatness.

One of my students was working as a waiter in the hotel, and to my surprise he appeared alongside of me. Tony responded very positively to him and the other young people around. It was obvious that he wanted to work with young actors, teaching them and working with them on material.

The evening seemed to end rather abruptly. Stella asked for the check, and shortly thereafter we vacated the room. As we left, she told us that we would be in touch. Tony wanted to come and work with my students. I told her that we were remodeling our theater and that as soon as it was finished we would be honored to have him come.

SIR ANTHONY VISITS MY THEATER

In February, several months after our Thanksgiving meeting, Anthony Hopkins, Stella and a large entourage descended on my little fifty-seat theater, which had been entirely remodeled. Though it had needed it, the fact that Sir Anthony was coming to work with my students had had a lot to do with how much we had improved the place. Eight or nine people came with Tony: his agent; the director of his upcoming film, *Hitchcock;* and several other people who were attached to him or the project. They all took seats in the first row.

I had invited all three of my classes to be there, so there was not an empty seat in the house. Tony was dressed casually and was sporting a brown hat like those worn in the fifties. We had talked about meeting for dinner before the event, in order to map out the evening, but that never happened, so I was planning to introduce him to my people, do a few instrumentals and a monologue, and then turn the session over to him. In order to discuss the program, Tony, Stella, my wife and I met in the office, which had been filled with flowers, finger sandwiches and a variety of soft drinks. I told them what I had planned to do, but Stella said that Tony had had a strenuous day and that they could not spend that much time there. She wanted him to just jump in, talk about himself, and then work with my people. Certainly I agreed.

When Tony mounted the stage, everyone applauded. He began by telling us that he had met the costars of the film he was preparing to do, Helen Mirren and Scarlett Johansson. He seemed quite impressed with having met them. When he started to address the group, he spoke about his early life, which was quite interesting. Some of what he shared he had already spoken about on Thanksgiving, but I enjoyed it as much the second time—his life as a boy in Wales, growing up during the war; how the soldiers, dressed in their uniforms, would come by his house with food and chocolates, which were unattainable in Wales in wartime; and how he loved most of all hearing stories about America and had always wanted to be here.

I looked at all of my students as they listened intently, and I was filled with warmth that washed through me like a current. I felt that I was giving them a beautiful gift. Tony also talked about Katharine Hepburn and again recounted how on his first day on the film she had said to him, "Don't act," and had walked away. He also described how powerful she was and how she would walk on the body of anyone who got in her way of achieving what she wanted. She had "a take-no-prisoners attitude towards life," he said. At one point he explained that with Marilyn Monroe the Method had gone out the window. At hearing that, my heart sank into my stomach. I have been a Method actor and teacher for over sixty years, and to hear Tony make that comment was very impacting. I have always thought that he is a great actor, and what he said didn't change my opinion; but it was very disappointing, since I know that the Method has been totally misunderstood for the entire century of its existence. At the origin, Stanislavski called his approach a "system." The term "method" was coined by Lee Strasberg. Actually, what the system, or Method, means is that the actor must, from the events of his own life, be able to experience from a real place the life of the character he is playing. I am positive that Sir Anthony does that intuitively. I know from things he said that he does a great deal of research on every character he plays, and as I told him at our first meeting, I do believe that he is the last of the great ones!

After his talk, Tony did a monologue. I don't know what it was from, but it was simple and subtly emotional, and the audience was completely involved in every word. At that point I felt that he was ready to start working with my people. The first person I called to the stage was a black actor named Jensen. He had been working on a monologue from *Guess Who's Coming to Dinner.* Tony jumped up onto the stage and waited for Jensen to start the monologue. After several lines he stopped him and began to make some suggestions about how to speak to the other character. He asked Jensen some questions about what he was communicating to his father. After answering them, Jensen reinvested in the monologue, which seemed more connected and real. Tony worked with Jensen for about twenty minutes, making suggestions and directing him. I could see that Jensen was both excited and intimidated, but he did the monologue with more depth and reality each time he reinvested in it.

The next group I called up to the stage consisted of three actors I had been working with in a scene from *The Glass Menagerie* between Tom, Amanda, and Laura, which they had done a couple of times in my Tuesday class. While it was a fairly long scene, I was confident that Tony would use as much of it as he chose to. They started the scene and did a few minutes of it, when Tony stopped them and began to work with Anna, who was doing Amanda. He asked her to walk away from Laura and talk to her as if she were looking out the window, and he gave her a few suggestions as to what she should be experiencing. The way he blocked it made it more interesting visually. After that he started working with Ross, who was doing Tom, and again he spoke to him about the content of what he should be experiencing, and he moved him around in an interesting way. Then he went to work with Renee, who was playing Laura, and also gave her several adjustments. He worked with all three of the actors for about half an hour. I thought that his work was very imaginative and helpful, although mostly directorial and somewhat different from the way I work with actors; but all three actors learned a lot from his work with them, and I was looking forward to their bringing the scene into class.

When Tony finished, Stella suggested that they call it a night. She talked to the group about her experience when studying with me and was very complimentary about my teaching. When they were leaving, Tony took an interest in one of my books that I had not already given him, so I made sure he had all seven of them. We hugged and said we would get together soon.

THE GLASS MENAGERIE AND BILLY HAYES

"OH LAURA...NOWADAYS THE WORLD IS LIT BY LIGHTNING! BLOW OUT YOUR CANDLES..."

It was 1953 or '54. I was working crew at Northwestern University on a main-stage production of *The Glass Menagerie.* Most of the actors in the play were students in the theater department, with the exception of an older actress, whom they had imported from somewhere in the Chicago area to play Amanda. They were all pretty good. My job was to pull a scrim curtain every time one of the characters walked from the dining room into the living room. As if by magic the scrim curtain would part. It was a directorial innovation, not indicated in the script. I fell in love with the play, promising myself that someday I would do it—act in it, produce it or direct it. I stood there in the dark, drinking in all the poetry behind every line and silently mouthing Tom's monologues. As he stood on the fire escape of the set, I silently said, "I didn't go to the moon. I went much farther. For time is the longest distance between two places." At the time I could have played Tom and in my imagination would have been wonderful.

Flash forward a few decades: I am now successfully teaching acting in Hollywood, have been for many years, and have directed some plays at the Actors Studio, where I met Joan Hotchkis and directed her one-woman play, *Legacy.* Joan was in my class and had done a couple of monologues from *The Glass Menagerie.* I thought that she was perfect to play Amanda, so I approached her to ask if she would be interested, if I could find a way to mount the play in Hollywood. She told me that she would. I cast all four roles out of my classes. Joan was a perfect Amanda. A seasoned actress, she had appeared on Broadway and in two television series, "The Odd Couple," where she played Tony Randall's girlfriend, and "My World and Welcome to It," where she was the female lead. Not only did Joan have the talent to play Amanda, but she also had a family background that paralleled where the character originally came from.

For Laura I used Erin Nico, an actor who, like a small bird, carried the vulnerable fragility that was Laura. She looked in a strange way very breakable and as if one would have to be careful around her. For Tom I originally cast Tony Marino who had a killer smile and a sensitivity that must have mirrored Tennessee Williams', whom the character was fashioned after. I rounded out the cast using Billy Hayes as the gentleman caller. Billy Hayes had come into my class a few years after escaping from a Turkish prison and writing *Midnight Express.* He had a full head of curly blond hair and an affable personality that totally fit the gentleman caller.

I like spending many months working on a play before it reaches the stage. We rehearsed in my theater studio, on the second floor of a building on La Brea Avenue. It was a horseshoe-shaped theater, where the seats bordered the stage area on three sides. We moved those seats back to give us more room, and we taped the floor to simulate the Wingfields' apartment: the living room, the dining room, and one of the bedrooms.

We worked on the play in my studio for about ten months before mounting it. During that period we strove to create parallel experiences to those of the characters. I went with Erin to find her glass menagerie. We visited many stores along Hollywood Boulevard, but I was careful not to influence her about her selections. I felt that they had to come from her. She selected a variety of glass animals: a horse, a deer, a small dog, a unicorn and a few others.

During rehearsal I had her share the stories she had made up about each of the figures. She was very imaginative, and as the rehearsals proceeded she was able to bond with those objects. It was important on an organic level for her to really have a relationship with each of them. We listened to recordings of the period, read Time-Life books about the Spanish revolution and the economy in America, about President Roosevelt and his fireside chats to the nation. I had Tony as Tom write poetry that he would read to Erin. In the play Amanda makes phone calls selling subscriptions to a woman's magazine to earn extra money, so I had Joan really calling people, attempting to sell subscriptions to a nonexistent publication; and when those people would hang up on her, she was really affected. Amanda is constantly talking about her earlier life and her popularity with the gentlemen callers, so I had Joan share her real experiences with her earlier courtships, while Tom and Laura would patiently listen, attempting not to be bored at hearing the same stories over and over. When the gentleman caller appears in the play, I had Billy do the same things: talk about his real ambitions and what he wanted to accomplish in his life. I was using the rehearsals to create authentic parallels in the lives of the actors.

A few months into rehearsal Tony came to me and told me that he wasn't comfortable with the character. He felt that he had trouble relating to him and wanted to bow out of the play. We were all very sad about his decision, but we had to honor it. It seemed to be a setback in our process, since relationships had already been established. I tried to understand Tony's decision and finally came to comprehend what had happened: Amanda and Tom are always in some sort of conflict with each other, and since we were working experientially, Joan and Tony were also experiencing conflict; and because Tony was so incredibly sensitive, he really incubated all of his hurt feelings. When acting isn't fun anymore, you bail!

I cast another of my students to play Tom—Richard Hatch, who later had a brief career on television and in films. He replaced Michael Douglas in "The Streets of San Francisco" with Karl Malden, and then he moved on to "Battle Star Galactica." Richard didn't have the same sensitive qualities as Tony, but he brought an ability to deal with Joan in a more theatrical way. The change in actors created a different quality in the piece, which I had to work very hard to integrate. About nine months had passed and I felt that the cast was getting anxious to do the play. I thought that we needed more time but decided to go with the will of the people.

We rented a theater, the Callboard Theater, a ninety-nine-seat Equity-waiver that was on an adjacent street off Melrose near La Cienega Boulevard. It was a very nice, well-appointed plant. We all pitched in to pay for the production, which ended up costing twenty-one thousand dollars. I hired Erik White, another of my students, who was a brilliant carpenter, builder, plumber and jack-of-all-trades, to build our set. Billy Hayes's wife, Wendy, stepped in and was our producer. Erik built an incredible set, replete with a real fire escape. Unfortunately, I felt we needed more rehearsal time before actually opening the play, so we used up about three weeks of our performance rental time.

As my memory serves me, about a week before we were to open, we received a letter from the people who held the rights to *The Glass Menagerie*, informing us that we had to stop the production immediately, because we hadn't been granted the rights to do the play. It was a huge blow, and we were all devastated. Billy said that Tennessee was fascinated by his story and had expressed interest in him, so he suggested that he should get on a plane, go see Williams and try to get his permission to do the play (see the excerpt from *Midnight Return* below).

When we finally opened, we received pretty good reviews and in some cases great responses. One evening, a well-dressed man, who looked as though he had appeared from a different era, walked into the lobby of the theater and asked if he could see the play. Vicki in the box office told him that we were totally sold out. Fortunately, I was standing in the lobby at the time. He said he was a close friend of Tennessee Williams and his neighbor in Florida. I told the stage manager to set up a chair for him and didn't even ask him to pay. When the play was over, he came into the lobby and called Tennessee Williams on the pay phone that was hanging on the wall. I listened to him as he spoke to Williams. He told him that it was the best production of that play he had ever seen, and as he reminded Williams, he had been at the opening night of the play on Broadway. He said this production was every bit as good and in some ways better. He urged Williams to get on a plane and come out and see it. I was blown away by the whole thing.

In the meantime we had used up all our rental time at the Callboard Theater, which had another show scheduled to come in, so we had to either close the show or move to another theater. That is not as simple as it may sound. Finding a theater that was available in our time frame and was suitable to our play was a difficult task. After an exhaustive search we found the Fountain Theater. It was not nearly as nice as the Callboard but it was an Equity-waiver theater, and we were desperate. The ceiling above the stage was too low to accommodate our set, so Erik had to cut the set down to fit. He did a magnificent job. No one would have guessed that the set had not been built for that theater. We only lost a week or so between shows and finished the run successfully.

Billy Hayes and Joan Hotchkis

MIDNIGHT RETURN

BY BILLY HAYES

(Before Billy Hayes came to work with me, his book Midnight Express *had been made into a movie. When I first met him, however, he was still shaken from his prison experience, so we worked together to eliminate the trauma. He once said that I, Eric, and his wife, Wendy, had saved his life. He has come a long way from that time to now, acting, directing theater and appearing in films. His second book,* Midnight Return, *was published recently, and he was very kind to give me permission to use an excerpt from it here.)*

By October of 1980 that's what I semi-seriously told people curious about my life after the *Midnight Express* madness. But I had become an actor, and for the past year now, Wendy and I had been working with Eric Morris and his small, tightly knit acting company in Los Angeles. We'd been rehearsing Tennessee Williams' classic play, *The Glass Menagerie.* Wendy was producing, and we'd raised money and made deposits on a theatre; in a week I was to make my theatrical debut as the Gentleman Caller.

Except that Tennessee Williams' agents had just denied us the rights to the play, which was why I found myself bleary-eyed and exhausted as the night flight from L.A. touched down in Miami. A slow-rolling wave of doubt washed over me, and I wondered what the fuck I was doing here. Was I really meeting with Tennessee Williams to ask his help in fighting ICM, the huge agency that represented him? Could I really pull this off, for myself and all the other actors depending on me?

I'd know soon enough, as I stumbled out to an old prop plane for the connecting flight to Key West. A crusty pilot in a rumpled blue uniform secured the door behind me once I entered the empty cabin. "Just us," he said, "might as well sit up front with me." Might as well, I thought, collapsing into the seat beside him. "Strap up good," he grinned, "this one should be a doozy."

My brain wasn't up to speed yet, but I didn't like the sound of that. I tried to ask him about a doozy, but my voice was drowned out by the rattling and clattering as we rumbled down the runway then lurched into the slick dawn sky. A little moan squeaked out of me, and I thought I heard the pilot laugh.

"Wheee," he said, as the plane bucked and shuddered. "You're lucky, this is probably the last flight out today, what with the turbulence." My stomach was full of wriggling eels.

"Turbulence? What turbulence?" I asked, shouting above the throbbing engines.

"That's the spirit," he cackled, mistaking my fearful question for bravado. "Hurricane Katrina, they're callin' her, building there beyond Cuba." I followed his gaze out the window to a line of huge dark clouds gathering like bull elephants on the horizon. "Should be here in forty-eight hours. Flights'll all be shuttin' down, 'fraid of the storm, but I love to fly in this weather." I was alone in the plane with this obvious lunatic, I had no parachute, and we were heading for the eye of a hurricane. All right, this was beginning to feel like Tennessee Williams' country.

An hour later we touched down on the tiny Key West runway. The air was thick, moist and fragrant. A soft drizzle began to fall as I cruised my rusty rented Honda past shabby houseboats snugged in along mangrove-lined lagoons on one side, and stately white houses wrapped with trellises of rampant red bougainvillea on the other.

On LaRue Street, beneath towering cypress trees, I rented a corner room off a wide veranda in an old mansion called the

Banyan House. I stripped off my damp clothes and stood beneath a slowly spinning ceiling fan, then collapsed onto the cool sheets of the four-poster bed. A saxophone was swaying softly somewhere nearby, and a faint drawling voice on a radio was speaking about a lady named "Katrina" building in the Gulf and heading for the Keys. Thunder rumbled in the distance, and on the slippery edge of sleep I laughed again to think that this was just like being in a Tennessee Williams play.

I woke at noon, surprised, covered with sweat, not a clue as to where I was. A lazy fan spun overhead. It was coming back now—I was in Key West to talk with Tennessee Williams. Was that right? Five years ago I'm in prison in Istanbul eating beans, and now I'm meeting America's greatest playwright? Strange transition.

I toweled off after a cold shower then found the phone number I'd gotten from Capt. Tony, an infamous Key West character who Wendy recently met on a film shoot about his exploits called *Key West Crossing.* Tony knew everyone and owned Capt. Tony's Saloon, where he used to drink with Papa Hemingway. When I called the number, a deep, cultured voice answered. It was Frank, Tennessee Williams' secretary/housekeeper. When I introduced myself he informed me "T.W." was at the doctor's and asked me to call back later. I set my alarm for four and plopped back into bed.

At four, T.W. himself answered. "Oh yes," he said, in soft, graveled-honey tones, "I remember you well, from the movie. You're beautiful." He'd confused me with Brad Davis, the actor who'd played me in the movie. I explained the difference and his voice flooded with emotion. "Oh, my child, you're the real one who was in that terrible prison?"

"Yes."

"Well, I truly feel for you and your family. I congratulate you on getting out." He began coughing and held the phone away from his mouth. "Excuse me, I'm not feeling too well today."

"Should I call back another time, sir?"

"Yes. Would you mind? Call me tonight at seven, after the news. I'm a news addict, so call me after the news at seven."

When I called at seven, T.W.'s speech was slurred, and he sounded drained. I could hear shouting in the background. "Billy, I am sorry, but there's some trouble here this evening. Let me call you tomorrow."

I was relieved. I'd rather meet him fresh, during the day. Capt. Tony had told me he was sharper by day, usually fried by sundown. I drove to Mallory Square, the southern tip of America, and watched a muted orange sun drown in dark purple clouds. I'd made contact with T.W., but I felt nervous and incomplete, and the storm was coming. I found an old, weathered phone booth on the worn wooden dock and called Wendy. I was reassured by the sound of her voice, but distressed to hear that we'd just paid $2,500 more to secure our rental of the Callboard Theatre and that the cast remained despondent because ICM still refused us the rights to *The Glass Menagerie.*

I felt pressured and fatigued as I walked back to the car. A steady rain began to fall, and the fleeting possibility of failure rippled like icy water down my spine. My uneasiness increased when I reached the car to find I'd locked the keys inside. All attempts to jimmy the door failed.

I huddled in the phone booth for an hour until a locksmith arrived and opened the door in a downpour. I drove to the Banyan House on automatic pilot then fell into a deep sleep and dreamed my father and I were together on a long, slow train...

Next morning, I had a late breakfast of croissants, coffee, orange juice, and anxiety beside the small, leaf-lined pool. I waited for the phone call while a mass of dark clouds loomed over the southern horizon. A large, tanned dumpling in a tiny black swimsuit tried to make conversation from the next lounge chair, but I politely ignored him, so he returned to the aging German countess lying topless beside him. I heard the mellow sax floating somewhere in the trees.

"That's the guy from Spyro Gyra," said Justin, the pool boy, swishing out from the house. He collected some dishes then struck a pose in front of us. "Anyone want anything?" he asked, with what had to be an Italian salami stuffed into his white string swimsuit. "No? Well, just call." And he was gone with a wink.

Noon passed. One o'clock. One-thirty. I called T.W.'s house. Frank answered—he was sympathetic and told me T.W. was lunching at the Pier House. My uneasiness increased. I decided action was called for and drove to the restaurant.

I saw T.W. at a far table with a solid, fiftyish blonde woman and an agitated young Englishman, whose long brown ponytail flopped about as he voiced his complaints in a cultured whine. "I've always been rich, goddamn it, and I've never been happy a day in my life!"

T.W. gently reached for his hand, but Ponytail shrugged him off and ranted louder. "I'm not a baby! Stop babying me!"

This seemed an inopportune time for introductions. I ordered coffee and watched from a nearby table. The Englishman raved on while T.W. listened patiently. He looked old and tired. He adjusted his thick, black horn-rimmed glasses, sipped some red wine, then rested his silvered beard on his hand. Just once his face lit up with a smile, and a deep, delicious laugh bubbled out of him.

When they rose to leave, Ponytail headed for the restroom and I hurried outside. T.W. emerged, a smallish figure with hands deep in his pea coat pockets and a little blue captain's cap snugged down on his white head. I stepped in front of him.

"Excuse me, Mr. Williams, I'm Billy Hayes."

He was startled, then recognized my name. "Oh, yes, forgive me for not calling you." I took his extended hand—it felt chilled and fragile.

"No, please, I apologize for intruding on you like this." We stared at each other a moment, then the blonde woman exited the restaurant and moved protectively to T.W.'s side. "Helen," he said, still holding my hand, "this is Billy Hayes."

"Ahh..." chimed Helen, relaxing, bathing me in a huge smile.

"Helen takes care of me," he offered. We stood there silently, and I could feel both of them examining me, sensing me with highly tuned antennae.

"I just need a moment, sir, to speak with you about *The Glass Menagerie*."

"Billy," said Helen, "why not follow us back to the house. You and Tom can sit by the pool and work this out."

T.W. nodded, still smiling at me.

Ponytail burst through the doors. There was a butter knife held low in his left hand. "Billy Hayes," Helen quickly began, "this is Robert—"

"Mister Robert Carroll," he shouted at me, "heir to the Carroll banking fortune, and I'm rich, bloody fucking rich!! Are you?!"

At lunch I'd noted the ferret-like movements of his thin body, and up close I could see his pupils were dark pinpoints. Still, I was surprised by his intensity and blurted out the first thing that came to me. "Well, I'm rich in spirit."

He sneered and said, "You look stupid," dismissing me with a glance and turning away. An adrenaline surge sent my right hand twitching toward his poncey little ponytail, but I checked the impulse. "And you look rude," I shouted at his retreating back. A quick glance showed me T.W. was aware of everything, intently focused on the scene.

"I look what?" said Robert, turning about.

"Rude," I replied, my body tensing for his response. The possibility of a fight was always a scary rush, even when you're dealing with a skinny junkie holding a butter knife.

"Of course I'm rude, you bloody fool, I can afford to be rude. It comes from being rich."

"It comes from being insecure."

He jerked as if stung by a bee. "I'm not insecure!" he screamed, waving the knife in the air. "I'm bloody fucking rich, and if you don't disappear instantly I'll cut your fucking balls off."

A sputter of sound from T.W.

"That's right, laugh, you bastard! You're loving this."

"Robert..." said T.W.

"Don't 'Robert' me! How'd you like it if I cut my bleeding throat with this knife? You'd be happy to be rid of me, wouldn't you?!" He wheeled around and charged back into the restaurant.

Helen took our arms and led us to a weathered little Datsun. "Robert has some problems," she said. "Just ignore him and follow us home. I'll distract Robert while you and Tom talk."

I crossed the parking lot to my car. Robert returned to the Datsun and sat up front beside Helen. There was shouting and loud arguing. As Helen got out and approached me, I knew the meeting was postponed again.

"I'm sorry," she said, "he's really impossible, and so draining on Tom. Could we meet you here at seven for dinner? We're putting Robert on the six o'clock flight."

I understood, I'd lived around junkies in prison. I looked to the dark sky and hoped Hurricane Katrina wouldn't close the airport. I looked back and Robert was sprinting wildly across the parking lot toward my car. He skidded to a halt just five feet from the driver's door and glared at me with crazed eyes. His thin body was quivering with rage. I cocked my left arm as he stepped toward the open window and hissed at me, "If I ever see your face around here again, I'll kill you!"

He leapt back as the door swung open and I surged out. I heard Helen shout, "Don't hurt him!" but I wasn't sure who she meant.

"Listen, Jack," I snarled, struggling for control, "you better find out who you're dealing with or you're gonna get hurt—bad!"

The effect on Robert was startling. All the tension left his body and a huge, silly smile creased his ascetic face. "Jack," he trilled, to no one in particular, "he called me... Jack!" Then he turned and floated serenely back toward the Datsun.

Katrina seemed to be lingering off Cuba. The muggy afternoon lay dead still awaiting her arrival. With time to kill before my dinner meeting with T.W., I found myself sitting against a towering magnolia tree beside a long rococo swimming pool in Ernest Hemingway's backyard. I was surrounded by cats—one hundred of them roamed the lush grounds around the vine-covered villa that was now a museum and tourist attraction. The kindly black guard at the front door had informed me the cats were all descendants of Papa's cats and were cared for according to instructions in his will.

I was the only visitor today. I'd just stood for an hour at the roped-off entrance to Papa's writing room, staring at the old Remington typewriter that sat faithfully on the high ledge of a massive wooden desk, awaiting the touch of a large man who worked standing on his feet. I wondered about inspiration, dedication, and the shotgun in Idaho.

It was quiet against the tree beside the pool. The water level was low and swampy, green with algae and fallen leaves. A small frog popped to the surface, then hopped up onto a mossy step. His googly eyes swiveled around, and we stared at each other before a gray cat leapt from the rhododendron bushes and pounced on the frog. The cat shifted its paws, and the frog splurted back into the pool. "Almost," I said to the cat, who took it well, settling down to stare at the water and wait.

"So, Billy," said T.W. a few hours later, as Helen helped settle him into a chair, "was it really as awful as the movie?" His bright blue eyes were bloodshot but alert behind the thick glasses. The Pier House was nearly empty, and a rising wind splattered occasional raindrops against the windows beside us. I was nervous and a little guilty about T.W. coming out in this weather.

"Well, emotionally it was pretty accurate, but they changed a lot of things."

"Yes, don't they always. You wrote the film?"

"No, sir, I wrote the book. Oliver Stone wrote the film."

"But all that happened to you?"

"Pretty much."

"The beatings and such?"

"Tom," intervened Helen, "maybe he doesn't want to talk about it."

"Oh, forgive me," said T.W., "I was just...curious."

"No, that's all right. I'm used to it. Everyone's curious."

"You were there how long?"

"Five years—from 1970 to 1975."

"My god. And didn't they send you to a madhouse where you killed that brutish guard and escaped?"

"The madhouse scene was very close to reality, but the escape was changed completely."

"So you didn't kill the guard and steal the keys?"

"No, sir, the guard was shot by another inmate a year earlier, and I escaped from a different prison, off an island in a rowboat in a storm."

"Your manners are impeccable, but do call me Tom."

"All right, Tom."

"Well, that ending certainly sounds more exciting and cinematic."

"It was. But Alan Parker, the director, wasn't interested in the escape as much as making a film about hope and fear and not giving up."

"I think he succeeded. Are you pleased with it?"

"Yes, for the most part. I have some problems, but I'm the least objective of viewers. The Turks aren't so happy."

"I should think not—they come across as quite barbaric."

"That's one of my main problems with the movie—you don't see a single good Turk, so they all look bad. Which, of course, isn't true."

"Of course." T.W. stared at me. "You certainly don't look like a hard-time convict. He has the face of an angel, doesn't he, Helen?"

"Yes," said Helen, smiling at me as I shifted around in my chair.

"And an athlete's body," said T.W. "Billy, I'd love to do a painting of you, naked beside the pool."

Naked beside the pool? Jesus! How much do I have to give for my art?

"I really should paint him, don't you think, Helen?"

"Yes, Tom, you should, but Billy, you have some problem with *The Glass Menagerie,* isn't that right?"

"Yes. We've been rehearsing for months—"

"Are you acting now?" asked T.W.

"Yes. This'll be my first time on stage—the Gentleman Caller."

"How wonderful."

"Except that we've put up money for the theatre and other expenses, and now we can't get the rights to do the play."

"Why not? It's done everywhere."

"I know, 281 times in the U. S. last year. Everyone loves your play—but our production is going to be different. The director, Eric Morris, has wanted to do a real version for twenty years, to show an Amanda with the guts to survive hard times alone with two children—"

"Are you always this hyper?" T.W. asked.

"I just think he's excited meeting you," said Helen.

"Yes, sir, it's really a thrill for me. I love your work...Tom."

"Thank you, Billy, your praise is gratifying, but do have some wine and relax. You can be a bit overwhelming."

"Sorry, I get revved up."

"I noticed. Robert usually out-blusters most people."

"I'm sorry if I caused problems."

"No, he's just insanely jealous and...sick."

"A lot of people were sick like that in prison. It makes life difficult."

"For everyone involved," said T.W., smiling at me. "And what are your indulgences these days?"

"Well, I did a lot of drugs back in the Sixties."

"Ah, yes, the Sixties, I've forgotten them well."

"But now I'm pretty straight, except for an occasional joint. Do a lot of long-distance running, marathons and stuff." I sipped some wine. "I don't even like alcohol, but it's an honor to drink with you."

That delicious laugh bubbled out of him again. "There are those who would consider it something less than an honor. You're very kind."

We sat quietly for a moment while the wind rattled the windows.

"So, are you a health nut? You certainly look healthy, doesn't he, Helen?"

Helen smiled at me. "You do look wonderful for having been in prison all those years."

"Well, I'm happy and in love and life is real sweet for me these days."

"What would you do," asked T.W. slowly, "if you knew you were going to die? Knew it. And very soon?" He fixed me with bright blue eyes, sunken now in the weathered folds of his face. I had a fleeting image of an old holy man sitting in a high mountain cave staring at a setting sun.

"I'm fascinated by death," I said. "What is it? What happens? I mean, I'm not ready to leave this yet, whatever this is, but I'm curious about what, if anything, is next. I figure it's something or nothing—and if it's nothing, you have nothing to worry about; and if it's something, then what is it?"

"It's nothing," T.W. said sadly.

"But what about our energy, our life-force continuing somehow, our body fading but our consciousness going on...?"

T.W. turned from the table as a hacking cough racked his body. After the spasm he asked, "Are you religious?"

"I was raised Catholic, but left the church after puberty created some major differences of opinion."

"It can certainly do that."

"I still have no use for organized religion, but I guess I'm more spiritual now."

"Spiritual...so you found God in prison?"

"Something like that."

"He seems to frequent those environs."

"Well, I got into yoga and meditation, learned about heart chakras and the God within all of us..."

T.W. let me prattle on awhile then gently asked, "How old are you?"

I suddenly felt quite foolish, and my embarrassment must have shown because he added, "That's all right, the Gentleman Caller is also an optimist."

"So why can't you do the play?" asked Helen.

"Right, the play, thank you. When we applied to the Dramatists Guild for rights, we were told ICM was considering a Tennessee Williams revival next year in L.A., so all rights were being withheld."

"They thought you'd be competition."

"Right, but we wouldn't be. This is a little Equity-waiver production! And besides, we love this play, we've been working on it in class for six months, we've paid for the theatre..."

"All right," said T.W., "calm down. It's just agents. Have you tried calling them?"

"I did. It took a while, but I got through and explained our situation. No one really cared."

"That's always the problem, isn't it? Well, don't worry, I'll call them, I'll talk with them."

That's what I wanted to hear! "So then I should wait until the Dramatists Guild contacts us about the rights?"

"Don't wait for anything!" shouted T.W., rising and leaning forward on the table. "I wrote the damn play and I'm telling you, do the play!"

"Yes, sir," I said, beaming, coming around the table to shake his hand and get embraced. His gray whiskers were brittle against my cheek, but there was still strength in his thin frame. He held me at arm's length and twirled a lock of my blonde hair on his finger. "Yes," he said, "I must paint you. Come to the house tomorrow for breakfast and I'll paint you beside the pool."

Hurricane Katrina was moving in, and the island was battening down when I arrived at T.W.'s house next morning. He was in his silk maroon robe and blue slippers and seemed to have taken a turn for the worse. I had my suitcase in hand and suggested cutting the meeting short. We embraced in the doorway and he said, "I'll have to paint you another time."

"I'd be honored." And I meant it. "Thank you."

"Well, God bless you and don't worry about anything. Just do the play."

I caught the last flight out, raced the storm to Miami and connected through to Los Angeles. Back at the theatre, everyone was excited by the news, and I felt the joy of an adventure completed.

A week later, two days before opening night, I was sitting alone on the steps of the Callboard Theatre during a rehearsal break when a telegram arrived from ICM. It informed us they'd been in touch with T.W. and that he now refused us permission to do *The Glass Menagerie* and that they were prepared to contact Actors' Equity and bend us over in court if we proceeded with our production. I walked back into the theatre, slowly crumpling the telegram into a small yellow ball.

"So, we ready to start again?" asked Eric, clapping his hands.

"Yeah, sure," I said, placing the yellow ball into the torn but neatly mended pocket of the Gentleman Caller's sport coat. "Let's do the play...do the play!"

We did the play. I never told the cast, we never heard from ICM, and there never was a revival in Los Angeles. The next time I saw T.W. was three years later—he was laid out in a coffin in a New York funeral parlor. I thought he looked good, at peace. I laid a rose in the coffin and whispered to him, "Something or nothing?"

(Years later Billy told me that he had received that telegram from ICM and that he had crumpled it, thrown it away and never mentioned it to anyone. We finished the run of the play to great reviews, which is a story in itself.)

EPILOGUE

I hope that the reader has enjoyed this book and has been enlightened and entertained by the stories in it. Since many of them are actually personal experiences of mine, writing the book felt like a trip down memory lane.

I would also like to thank all those who contributed to the book with their wonderful stories. I will always be grateful for their generosity and their friendship.

I have spent sixty-five years in Hollywood and over the years have taught upwards of thirty thousand people, many of whom you will never hear of. A great number of them left the pursuit of acting, because they were too sensitive to endure the whips and scorns of an industry that is primarily a business for making money. There is very little loyalty and even less concern for the actor's journey. My heart goes out to every actor who has trodden on the path. As a teacher, I count my victories as much for those who sought another path as for those who succeeded as actors.

As for myself I have been extremely fortunate and have had a very fulfilling career. I thank God that instead of looking into a mirror and only seeing my own reflection, the mirror turned into a clear window through which I saw the world and all the wonderful things in it.